Private Prayers in Public Places

To the Thornton

with best wishes!

Private Prayers in Public Places

✦

The Notebook of an Urban Pilgrim

Donald G. Shockley

iUniverse, Inc.
New York Lincoln Shanghai

Private Prayers in Public Places
The Notebook of an Urban Pilgrim

iUniverse, Inc.

For information address:
iUniverse, Inc.
2021 Pine Lake Road, Suite 100
Lincoln, NE 68512
www.iuniverse.com

ISBN: 0-595-30232-7

Printed in the United States of America

In loving memory of my dear friend

James B. (Jim) Ifft

By listening deeply to the message of any given moment I shall be able to tap the very Source of Meaning and to realize the unfolding meaning of my life.

David Steindl-Rast, *A Listening Heart*

Contents

Preface

The Introduction that follows will spell out in more detail how the individual meditations in this book came to be written in public places and why I call them prayers. But at the outset, it is important for the reader to understand that this writing occurred in an unplanned fashion over a period of more than twenty-five years. Beginning in the late seventies, I developed the habit of writing as a way to pass the time when I was traveling or otherwise in a situation that involved waiting. Usually the writing was in the form of a response to whatever I saw and heard around me. Eventually, a friend of mine who was aware of this practice invited me to read some of the prayers at a banquet associated with a lecture series at the University of Redlands. Since then, I have given readings on a number of occasions and, invariably, folks ask for copies of the prayers or urge me to publish them. Once I decided to put them together in the form of a book, some difficult questions arose.

What, if anything, unites all these bursts of writing in public places? In what order should they be presented? Should I just string them together like a series of poems, or should I try to group them in some way? If the latter, should they be set into chronological order or what? In the final analysis, I decided to arrange them into a sequence that is part autobiographical, part geographical, part chronological, part topical and so on. The introductory narratives for each section are autobiographical in character and therefore basically chronological. But some time jumps are allowed in order to bring together topically related pieces. A reader might do well just to pick one of the prayers from the table of contents and go directly to it. Then read another one or two before coming back to read the Introduction to the whole collection. The point is that although I have made an effort to provide a connected framework, the prayers were nevertheless written in a random fashion and could be read that way.

I felt it important to identify the year in which each selection was written as well as the place. Many of the locales will be familiar to readers, (e.g. Chinatown in San Francisco, Times Square in New York, Peachtree Street in Atlanta) and already having some images in mind should enhance the enjoyment of the prayers. In some cases the location no longer exists and a glance at the year in which a piece was written may clear up questions about that. For example, both

Brother Juniper's Restaurant and the Hot Cookie Corner in Atlanta have been gone for years. But some will remember them. Likewise, there is no Pacific Southwest Airlines today, but its planes were once a common sight in the sky over California.

I assure any skeptical reader that these pieces, almost without exception, were indeed written in the places indicated. Some have been re-written again and again, but always with the intent of drawing out the meaning implicit in the original experience. In some cases I have changed details in the interest of avoiding the extremely remote possibility that a specific person might be recognized in one or more of the prayers.

On those occasions when I have gone intentionally to some particular place with the idea of writing a new piece of this kind, I have invariably found disappointment. This taught me that the element of surprise is essential; something in the environment has to speak to me and I have to listen and wait for the words to come. When this process really "works" the words seem to be given and hardly mine at all. For this reason, I can read over and over again what I have written and still discover levels of meaning that I had not recognized before. But it is the responses of persons who have heard or read some of the prayers that have given me the courage to share them with a wider audience. I express my gratitude here, and in the acknowledgements at the end of the book, to all who have encouraged me to write. I am especially grateful for the many strangers whose words and actions in public places have provided windows through which I have caught fleeting glimpses of that other Presence "in whom we live and move and have our being" (*Acts* 17:27-28).

Introduction

If your mother loves you too much you eventually have to say *no* to her. It is the only way you can remain comfortable at home. Something of the sort was going on with me when I was young. Not with my real mother, but with the religious ethos that had created me and nurtured me to young adulthood. When a good college taught me to think critically, I had to say *no* to some aspects of the religious experience that had made me who I was. As one example, the language of personal piety no longer rang true to me and I had to stop using it. This meant that prayer as I had always known it (asking God for favors) was no longer available to me. But in my youthful quest for theological integrity, I surrendered an important spiritual resource. This book is the story of how I got it back or, to tell the truth, how it got back to me. Once I stopped talking to God, God started talking to me. What God said to me was that if I wanted to learn how to pray again, I would have to stop talking and start listening.

When I first began to assert my spiritual independence my mother, the church, responded boldly. She appointed me to serve as pastor of a small rural congregation. It was the moral equivalent of teaching a child to swim by tossing him into the deep end of the pool. I had just finished my first year in college! So many years later, that audacious act still seems incredible to me. At the beginning of my sophomore year in college, at the tender age of nineteen, I was appointed the sole minister of a rural church in Alabama and served in that capacity for the next three years. It was not a responsibility I sought or even saw coming. Months earlier, I had inquired about the possibility of locating a part-time job as a youth director in a local church. The next thing I knew, the Methodist powers in the area had made me the spiritual leader of the Woodstock Methodist Church, about thirty miles from the campus. Abruptly, it became my responsibility to stand before a small congregation of intelligent and faithful people and deliver a sermon every Sunday morning and every other Sunday night. During those three years I more or less backed into a form of spiritual discipline which for a long time I did not recognize as prayer.

From Sophomore Pastor to Chief Expecter

As a student pastor attempting to cope with the twin pressures of academic work and sermon preparation, I formed the unfortunate habit of finishing my sermons on Sunday mornings. Often, ideas that had seemed promising earlier in the week began to look more and more empty as the week progressed. Many Saturday nights I went to bed thinking I still had nothing worth saying. But when Sunday dawned it was a do or die situation. Facing a forty-minute drive in addition to the final preparation, I would be out of the dormitory by six o'clock and on my way to a local donut shop where a cup of coffee would jolt my head awake. Before long I discovered that I could work rather well right there at the counter and I was soon jotting down notes as I sipped the coffee. This public place, being neither church nor campus, curiously freed my mind from the distractions associated with those more familiar environments. Eventually, this coffee shop interlude became a kind of ritual and, finally, a completely necessary step in the process of getting ready to speak, regardless of how well prepared I was beforehand.

Although, thankfully, it has not always been on Sunday mornings, this habit of writing in public places has continued to the present. I often hear or see things in public environments that make a direct contribution to what I am thinking about at the time. And so it happened that I began to anticipate such episodes and found myself going into public places in a mood of openness and expectation. Regardless of whether or not I had a sermon to prepare, being an anonymous presence in a public place began automatically to raise my awareness of everything and everybody around me. And, somehow, the situation would eventually speak to me. I can demonstrate how this often works.

Many years ago now, during the season of Advent, I sat at the counter of a sandwich shop in my hometown of Birmingham, Alabama. I had been there for half an hour, attempting to get started with a sermon for the season, when a waitress who had been observing my note making with growing apprehension confronted me with an accusation. I was, she charged, an undercover agent for the parent company, sent to evaluate employee performance. When I had reassured her, without divulging my real business, she turned to leave me. And, with a marvelous slip of the tongue, she exclaimed, "Well, I'm sure glad you're not one of those *expecters.*" I could have jumped for joy! "Dear lady," I wanted to say, "I am in fact *the chief expecter*! It is my job to go into places like this and expect someone to tell me something of spiritual significance. And you have met my expectations extraordinarily well!"

The waitress gave me a timely reminder of the appropriate mood of a Christian preparing for the coming of Christmas, and the recounting of the exchange between us became the cornerstone of my sermon. More importantly, she nudged me forward into a new stage of appreciation for the capacity of an ordinary situation to speak to anyone who is prepared to listen and look. From that day onward I would *expect* to hear interesting and profound things in public places; I would *expect* strangers to teach me, to evoke from my consciousness surprising affirmations of life. I then knew beyond doubt that a mysterious dimension of depth, present in all human situations, would reveal itself in direct proportion to my readiness to receive it.

A Curious Way To Pray

Brother David Steindl-Rast, a monk of the Benedictine order has written, "By listening deeply to the message of any given moment I shall tap the very Source of meaning and the unfolding meaning of my own life." My experience strongly suggests that this is true. When observed carefully, ordinary moments often become metaphors: they are what they are, but they also bear within them a reference to larger and deeper meanings. This listening to ordinary moments is the primary form which prayer has taken in my life. If the forms of spiritual expression I knew as a child encouraged me to look away from Earth toward heaven, I gradually recognized that the only way I could see heaven was to look more closely at Earth.

Writing is a necessary sequel to this special way of listening and looking. It brings images and metaphors to the surface and gives them form before they get away. So I write while still in the public space, in an almost stream of consciousness fashion, letting the thoughts come as they will. In addition to coffee shops, the following meditations were written in airplanes, on trains, in a variety of waiting rooms, in museums, and on at least one occasion while watching a baseball game. I welcome the observation that these writings of various lengths are a *curious* way to pray. The word *curious* has its roots in a Latin word which means both to care and to cure. The relationship between caring and curing is obvious enough, but how are they both related to curiosity? To be curious is to "pay attention." That is what these meditations represent: a way of paying attention which is open and ready to receive whatever comes in the encounter with people, places and things. It is prayer as listening and looking. It is a spiritual practice which is available to anyone who is blessed with the gifts of seeing and hearing, and no doubt to others who may enjoy means of perception which I do not yet understand.

Why Share These Private Thoughts?

The sharing of this work is on one level an exercise in autobiography. But why would I assume that these odd bits of private reflection might be of interest to anyone other than myself? Carl Rogers, founder of an approach to psychological counseling called client-centered therapy, once said that what is most personal is most universal. It is fair to say that—as a consequence of my vocation—I have read more, traveled more, and done more public speaking than most people have. But in our development as human beings, we all go through common experiences and face many of the same questions. Every adult was once an infant, once a child, once a teen-ager, and so on through the stages of life. We all go through the critical transitions from one stage of life to the next. While our circumstances are immensely varied, these transitions force upon every one of us crises of identity and meaning. And we inevitably look to each other to find alternative ways of understanding and interpreting our experiences. We have no other models. The possibility and promise of such mutual support is the idea that motivates me to share what I have written.

Every life provides a testimony concerning the meaning of the whole human enterprise, and is therefore worthy of study from a theological perspective. But we often do not realize that the life story we have most access to is our own. It is possible, especially as we get beyond the midpoint of our lives, to examine the particular story which is unfolding in us and through us. Although this "research" is not undertaken in an orderly fashion, I am nevertheless looking for clues to the great Mystery by laying out random bits of evidence from my own experiences while riding the roller coaster of life. In reading all together what I have written on napkins, place mats, grocery sacks, barf bags on planes, in the margins of brochures and on yellow legal pads, I recognize some of the dominant themes which have shaped my life experience. And, following Carl Rogers' observation, I trust that these themes will strike a responsive chord in the thoughts and feelings of others. More importantly, I hope what I have shared will encourage others to discover that writing is an important resource for the spiritual life.

The inexplicable reality of universal human suffering comes up again and again in what I have written over so many years. But I am no closer to a morally acceptable explanation of evil than I was when I was in college. My thinking about this topic always ends in ambiguity if not in paradox. But I am nevertheless a prisoner of hope. I find reassurance in images from the Bible and in the goodness and beauty which greet us every single day. Sometimes, eucharistic images (the bread and wine of Holy Communion) surprise me, jumping out in the midst of everyday situations. And, of course, light is the most powerful metaphor we have. I invite the reader to look for these images and to notice also how helpful it is to be keenly aware of children in public arenas. Finally, I feel the need to say that there is a fair amount of humor in these prayers that I hope will be recognized as such. The poet Robert Frost said that a poem begins in delight and ends in wisdom. I am not a poet and I make no claim to wisdom. But I do have a capacity for delight and I hope *that*, as much as anything else, is what comes through in these pages.

I.

I Changed My Mind in San Francisco

Although my application to begin doctoral studies had been accepted, as my last year in seminary drew to a close I was invited to join the staff of a large suburban church in Birmingham, Alabama. It was a good opportunity and I decided to go home. But after serving two years during the time when our city was one of the hottest spots in the civil rights movement, I concluded that I was not cut out to be an effective pastor. Again I applied for admission to graduate study even though I knew that I should stay in Birmingham. The issue was settled by an unexpected opportunity to serve as college chaplain at my alma mater across town (Birmingham-Southern College). I took the job and remained in the position for eight years. In spite of, or perhaps because of, the social turbulence and violence that racked Birmingham during those years, it was a period that settled my vocational direction for the rest of my life.

I have lived at the intersection of faith and learning for as long as I can remember. Serving as pastor of a rural church while at the same time experiencing the shaking of the foundations which an excellent liberal arts education cannot fail to produce determined the course of my life. In spite of strong reservations about my suitability for the formal role, I have never lost the heart and instincts of a pastor, attributes that were already apparent in my childhood. At the same time my educational experience kindled a flame of intellectual curiosity which has never gone out. If the phrase "faith seeking understanding" (and sometimes the reverse) was to be the theme of my life, what better place to spend it than in religious leadership on college and university campuses?

Still having the desire for doctoral studies, but unwilling to leave either my job or Birmingham, I eventually discovered that the San Francisco Theological Seminary had just the opportunity I was looking for. It would require eight years of directed study including two summers and a full twelve months in residence, but somehow with the support of my college and the Danforth Foundation I managed to do it. Going from Birmingham to San Francisco in the sixties was like falling asleep one night and waking up the next morning on another planet. My first encounter with the place was in the summer of 1967, the year in which the culture of flower power was at its zenith. Experiencing that city any time would have been a transforming experience for me, but there I was in the midst of what seemed, however briefly, to be a genuine revolution of consciousness which would sweep through America and possibly the whole of western civilization.

Much to the consternation of some, when I returned to Birmingham I brought some San Francisco with me. It only got worse after my second summer there. My alma mater now had a chaplain decked out in a beard, boots, bellbottoms and flower print blouses, and who drove his family around in a Volkswagen van festooned with flower and ladybug decals. For the most part, the students seemed to love these external adaptations in the customary image of a man of God. But the real changes were taking place inside me. It is almost embarrassing to talk about it now, but there was an exhilarating sense that liberation from all sorts of repression was now possible; it was "blowing in the wind." All sexual hang-ups would disappear, oppressed minority groups would receive just treatment, mainstream culture would welcome diversity, wars would cease, and so on. Most of these hopes were ground into dust by the course of events, but—nevertheless—things would never be entirely the same again for me.

After those initial experiences in San Francisco, I was granted a sabbatical leave and moved there with my family for a full year as the seventies began. In 1971, we went back to Birmingham for a year then moved to southern California where I served for seven years as chaplain of the University of Redlands. During those years there were many visits to the San Francisco Bay area and for a long time afterward professional and personal travel took me there from time to time. For a pilgrim who looks for evidence of the Spirit in whatever city he visits, San Francisco is a rich site indeed.

1. I Saw the Light

I am always surprised by the quality of the light in northern California. Today, here at the University of California at Berkeley, it seems unusually vivid somehow. I suppose it is not correct to say that one sees the light itself; one sees its effects in the very distinct appearance of the things it illumines. The shadows are sharp-edged and the flowers virtually shine in their splendor. The sky is August azure, and the sun is warm and friendly. What creates this difference in the quality of the light? Is it the relative absence of humidity? Is it the clearness of the sky, or the nearness of the sea? There is probably a simple answer, but I do not know what it is.

I first visited this spot fourteen years ago, and I suppose I came just to see the place that was ground zero for the cultural explosion of the sixties. Over the years since, I have come back at least a dozen times, and although the scene keeps changing there are always reminders of its past. Today, in the wide, red brick expanse of Sproul Plaza, for example, a man—rotund and forty-ish—sits in an attitude of prayer smack in the middle of this vast open space. Were it not for his wooly black beard he would provide a passable image of the Buddha himself. But I am more interested in a tiny girl no more than two years old who tries earnestly to escape her mother's grasping hand: she breaks free and runs, falls, rises undaunted, but is soon re-captured and compelled to move in the direction from which she came. She responds by first going limp in every joint then stiffening into a howling rage when she is scooped up and carried away, wisps of fine golden hair accentuating her precious, innocent head like a halo. She is an angel in spite of herself.

Across the way, I can see a priest standing in the midst of a circle of attentive people and speaking in an animated fashion. The sight reminds me of the street preachers who were here routinely a dozen years ago and I move nearer to the group to hear what he is saying. But I quickly discover not only that he is speaking in French, but also that his audience is not made up of students but of elderly people who crane their necks to see whatever it is that is attracting his frequent gestures. The cameras hanging from loops around their necks confirm that this is a tour group of some kind. But the scene nevertheless leaves me remembering a man named Hubert who would show up on this spot in the sixties to preach to small clumps of students who loved to heckle him. One day I heard him conclude one of his harsh homilies by telling such a group that they were all lost and headed straight to Hell. But it was clear that Hubert was enjoying the encounter as much as the students were. Even when he said such things, he could not manage to extinguish the twinkle in his eyes or the half-grin on his face. And when at last he turned to leave, the students would cry, genuinely I think, "Don't go, Hubert; please come back!" Beneath the mutual mocking, there was some kind of quest, some longing to really know and be known across a rather wide chasm of class and culture.

I suppose it is my vocation to see signs of the Spirit everywhere I go, but here in Berkeley I could not suppress the thought if I tried. The student rebellion has gone away and the world is not noticeably better than it was before. Nevertheless, the light continues to shine. Still the sun watches and warms this motley crew of folks flowing back and forth along Telegraph Avenue, onto Sproul Plaza and through the Sather Gate.

The University of California at Berkeley, 1981

2. The Old Rollin' Cross

At first glance you would have to surmise that Jesus just crossed a busy street in San Francisco. That is not exactly what occurred, but that is the way the unusual sight initially appeared. I am sitting at the bar of the Buena Vista, the place where Irish coffee made its first appearance in this country. On a Friday afternoon the place is packed and I have taken up a position where I can watch the people inside and also have a good view of folks outside as they come up the hill from Fisherman's Wharf.

Across the street scores of people wait for a chance to ride the signature emblem of this city, the famous cable cars. Out of the midst of them just a moment ago there emerged a bearded young man of quite serious demeanor. Across his shoulder lay a heavy wooden cross that I judged to be about eight to ten feet in length. A considerable burden, I first thought, if he expects to negotiate the hills around here on foot. Anyway, I watched as this surrogate Jesus stood among the multitudes waiting for electronic permission to cross the street in my direction. As he came into full view, I was startled by what I saw.

Fixed to the foot end of the long vertical member of the cross was a very nice spoked wheel, thickly rimmed with rubber. The wheel was about eighteen inches in diameter, suggesting somewhat the basic feature of a unicycle. Anyway, the young man's grimness not withstanding, one had to conclude that this particular cross moved along quite smoothly. Around me in the Buena Vista, there were a few comments on the absurdity of the sight, but most of my fellow patrons either failed to notice or were not all that impressed.

This episode seems to suggest that, if the Lord Jesus returns to earth, San Francisco should be seriously discounted as a possible point of entry. Not enough people would notice is the way I have to think about it. But I will tell You this much: I, at least, will be both awake and alert. I am always on the lookout, and I am ready to spot You in any guise, including that of a confused young man carrying a uniquely mobile cross. You just go ahead and come whenever the notion strikes. If I have occasionally expressed doubts about Your returning to us it is only because I have never been sure that You left. Anyway, I like to hang out in places like this where I can have a good view of the people, and I am watching. Almost always, I am watching.

The Buena Vista, San Francisco, 1981

3. Fiddler on the Street

The corner at San Francisco's Powell and Market streets has long been the scene of characters seeking to work the crowd of pedestrians and cable car riders in one way or another. Today I stood for twenty minutes or so observing the contrast between a street musician and a woman preacher as they pursued their strikingly different objectives.

The fiddler filled the air with warm and joyful sounds as appreciative pedestrians paused for a few moments to listen and drop coins into the waiting instrument case at his feet. The old lady, moving in a mental world of her own, paced about with glassy eyes, preaching defeat and doom to one and all. She would allude occasionally to biblical episodes, but for the most part she just accused us all of having misplaced our confidence in the usual catalogue of Satanic allurements: money, privilege, status, self-indulgence.

While this well-intentioned prophet was no doubt correct in her analysis of our individual failures, she scarcely served as a convincing witness to a better way. Soon she launched into a sadly comic attack upon the Roman Catholic Church, saying that children in parochial schools learn filthy language from their teachers. She had personally been the object of unspeakable obscenities hurled by a passing nun!

Meanwhile, the fiddler played his warm melodies and, from the look of his tattered clothes, he, at least, had not yet been victimized by riches. And he chose not to condemn the world, but to stand where it passes by and surround it with a song.

Pacific Southwest Airlines, 1977

4. A Moving Experience

When a poet asks, "What is so rare as a day in June?" I have to answer by saying that if that day in June is spent in San Francisco with no personal agenda to speak of, there is no day more rare. This day, at least, promises to be perfect. It is only eight o'clock in the morning and I have already taken a leisurely stroll through Chinatown on my way to an Italian bakery on the other side. There, I read the *San Francisco Chronicle* while I sipped a cappuccino and savored every bite of an apple pastry. Now I have wandered on down to Washington Square and taken a perch on a green bench to survey the Saturday morning scene. The gleaming white Church of St. Peter and St. Paul catches the morning light and sends it down to bless with serenity this tiny urban oasis. Certainly all is not well with the world, or even with San Francisco. But you could not prove it here at this moment.

On a stretch of grass some sixty yards in front of the church a man I would judge to be in his sixties is engaged in some sort of slow motion exercise. It first appeared that he was trying to communicate with someone via slow motion semaphore, but without the flags. His yellow shorts and blue tee shirt suggest that he is costumed for physical exertion, but there is nothing aerobic about this activity; it is much too slow. What would one call it? It is not dance unless one can dance without moving one's feet very much. Whatever it is, it has now drawn the attention of two early rising tourists who have trained their cameras on the man. What will they tell the folks back home when this particular slide hits the screen? That it is further evidence that weird things occur routinely in San Francisco? That is not the way I assess the scene. I am bound to think so, of course, but I would say that this man in motion is using his body to get in touch with his soul.

On the other side of the quadrangle a dozen or so elderly Chinese women are bending their backs and stretching their arms and legs. Some stand and swing first one leg and then the other, back and forth in pendulum fashion while others appear to march in place with a bent-knee kick preceding each step. These motions say clearly that their concern is with their bodies, how to keep the vital juices flowing, muscles toned and ready when needed to negotiate the physical challenges of an elderly person's ordinary day.

More people are showing up and all but me seem to be focused on motion in a variety of modes. A jogger moves around the perimeter of the park, a child is chased by her brother in an erratic pattern and, as if to join the fun, a pigeon flies a sudden low diagonal path through this space. Across the way, the slow motion man continues the flowing movements of his body as though he hears a gentle and soothing melody that is inaudible to the rest of us. So what is the message of these Saturday morning moments? Somehow the beauty of living bodies in movement speaks to the hunger of my heart to let the Spirit flow freely in myself. That is not to suggest that the Spirit and I are strangers to each other. She approaches the windows of my mind frequently and I always open them wide when I hear Her outside. But somehow I've got to open doors to the rest of me until my entire being resonates with the Song that makes the whole creation move.

Washington Square, San Francisco, 1980

5. A Place With No Name

This summer Sunday in San Francisco is cold and windy. A low-lying fog has silently crept in from the sea to shield the city from the light and warmth of yesterday's brilliant sun. When I left the hotel this morning, I was on my way to church, but I never got there. The chill and grayness of the morning penetrated to my insides and all I wanted to do was wander about in a kind of melancholy mood and think things over. I am not sad or depressed by any means; I *like* an overcast day and I like to be surprised by what the weather decides to do. Perhaps the best word for my activity today would be *brooding*. Although the term has a kind of dismal quality, its basic reference is to a process that leads to new life: a mother hen nestling eggs beneath her wings.

I started this day with a walk through Chinatown, beginning at Union Square, then ambling north along Stockton Street toward the bay. Early in the morning it is possible, if you are a white boy from Alabama, to walk for blocks without seeing or hearing anyone who looks or sounds like you. I like to listen to Chinatown and as I ate breakfast in a bakery I heard not a word of English. Even though you know that all those energetic sounds in this commercial district must have a highly pragmatic intent, they still sound like music to me. Precisely because I do not understand the words, the Chinese language surrounds me like a blanket and, stupidly I suppose, it makes me feel shielded and safe. It may simply be the case that it makes clear to me that I am not at home and not at work; nobody here has any expectation of this stranger in their midst and I am therefore free from the normal concerns of a typical day in my life.

When I left the bakery I had an encounter that seemed very strange to me. Weaving my way here and there along the already crowded sidewalks of the community, I came upon a funeral cortege in process of formation in the street. I am not talking about cars, but about people preparing to walk in parade to honor and mourn the passing of a relative or friend. As I stood, puzzled by the notion of beginning a day with a focus upon death, I distinctly heard a cock crow! Around the corner a few moments later, I discovered an old woman and a boy selling live fowl from the back of a pick-up truck: chickens, ducks and squab. Perhaps it was the cackle of a hen I heard and it was the morbid setting that made it sound to me like the rooster sent to prick the conscience of the apostle Peter on that fateful morning long ago. In this case the sound came from a creature far more concerned about its own fate than mine.

Eventually I made my way to the water and as the fog began to lift, I boarded the Golden Gate Ferry to cross the picturesque bay to Sausalito, a crescent-shaped resort town on the other side. During the ride one can see the Golden Gate Bridge and Alcatraz Island together, one a powerful symbol of freedom, the other of bondage. How doubly bitter it must have been to look at the graceful sweep of the bridge through a barred window. The island prison was noted for its ability to allow no escape, while the bridge, as its name implies, holds out the promise of liberty to those arriving in America for the first time or returning home safely from foreign wars.

Anyway, I have finally come to the No Name Bar in Sausalito. It actually has a sign out front with nothing on it; that's how you know you have come to the right place. I have chosen the small courtyard in the back, cozily closed in by vines above, rocks and flowers to the sides. I like the hiss of the gas heaters overhead that break the chill when needed. And I like to sit here as I am doing now, nursing an Irish coffee, looking back at the day and writing whatever comes. I did not intentionally set out to come here; it is just the place I gravitated to after all the walking and riding.

Perhaps a place with no name is where I belong today. Who am I anyway, and what am I trying to do? I have an important meeting in the city tomorrow and then, I suppose, what usually passes for my identity will snap back into place. But, sometimes, the Mystery that lives beneath the surface of ordinary days makes an audible whisper, calls us to see beyond the appearance of things. I love it when that happens. But I hasten to say that there is nothing about a monastic life that would appeal to me; I would not want to focus on these matters every day. My urge is not to withdraw from everyday life but to savor it to an extraordinary degree. So I am grateful for rare days like this when I can wander about and receive the sights and sounds of such an interesting and beautiful city. For a while, at least, nobody knows my name and I begin to forget it myself. And I catch a fleeting glimpse of that playful Presence that flits away whenever I get too close. She always runs away, but not before imparting yet again the sense that something is trying to happen inside me. And I know it is the same something that wants to happen in everyone else and in the whole creation. Something new and precious waits to be born and I am trying to get my wings around it.

The No Name Bar, Sausalito, California, 1980

II.

A Young Man Goes West

After spending a full year in San Francisco as the seventies began, I came home to realize that I could now leave Birmingham with a clear conscience and make a fair number of powerful people happy in the process. The college had fallen on hard times and, in my absence, the meager resources of the chaplain's office had been raided for use elsewhere. It seemed to me that an important chapter in my life had ended and a new one was waiting to begin. When an invitation came to join the University of Redlands, in southern California, I knew it was time to go.

The decision to pull up our very deep roots in Alabama was not an easy one. Vocationally, the job—being chaplain of another outstanding liberal arts college in a different region of the country—seemed to be made to order, but the other dimensions of the move were not so clear. Could we actually leave our families and a nurturing web of life-long friendships? We did not know a single soul in the Southwest. Nevertheless, the day came when our family of five, plus two cats, piled into the aforementioned Volkswagen van and headed west.

It was during our seven years in southern California that I first met Howard Thurman. This great African American preacher and mystic, already advanced in age, stayed three weeks on the Redlands campus rather soon after I arrived. We became well acquainted during that time and on other occasions when he returned for speaking engagements. Although we did not see each other often, we stayed in touch over the years until his death. I do not know how to measure his influence in my life, except to say that it was more personal and spiritual than academic even though he wrote many important books. I was especially taken by the way he combined in himself a capacity for deep reflection and an almost impish sense of humor. As the years go by my sense of his influence in my life only gets stronger, and I am deeply grateful for it.

During the time I spent in Redlands, I was also intrigued by a method of journal writing being developed by the psychologist Ira Progoff and I attended a few of his workshops. He had formulated techniques for writing about personal experiences that seemed to open deeper levels of consciousness. It was a method that grew out of his early years as a therapist who had artists among his clients. The basic idea involves writing dialogues. For example, if you write an imaginary dialogue with a person, a place or even a thing—such as a work of art—you will be surprised by some of the words and images that appear as you write both sides of the conversation. Although I did not recognize it at first, I believe that my meditation and writing in public places, which I had long practiced, came under the influence of both Howard Thurman and Ira Progoff during the years I spent in Redlands.

The following prayers are among those I wrote while living in southern California in the late seventies. I hope you can recognize the humor as well as the pathos in them. There is pathos aplenty as I reflect on my last year at Redlands during which I was asked to be provost rather than chaplain. I was the chief academic officer in a time of turmoil for the university and therefore suddenly moved from being someone who alleviated pain to someone who caused it by making hard but necessary decisions. It became acutely clear to me why the root meaning of the word *decide* is "to cut off." Those who have responsibility for institutions and therefore have to balance the claims of the future with those of the present moment, and to face the necessity of comparing the corporate welfare with the interests of individuals, know very well that to decide is to swing a two-edged sword that nearly always wounds the one that wields it. While a university chaplain's life is far from easy, an academic administrator's day involves difficulties of a different sort. Looking back, I can see that the experience was good for me and, since the institution is thriving today, I suppose I did no lasting damage.

A chaplain colleague of mine used to say, "The situation is hopeless, but not serious." For him, that was a theological assessment of the relationships among human beings in institutional settings. And it always reminded me that human beings are born to laugh or at least to smile. Since humor is a gift from God, it is sometimes permissible to be playful when we are prayerful. So be prepared for some prayers which hover on the brink of irreverence as well as those which constitute an inner cry of anguish.

1. Playing With Praying

Day giving way to night on an early summer evening in this desert climate provides pleasant sense experiences. In the afternoon the temperature reached into the nineties, but as the blazing sun dropped from view the waning light seemed to absorb the warmth, casting first a rose, than a purple hue across the mountains. A steady, gentle breeze has come up and is pressing our faces with an almost neutral force: it is very dry, this wind, and neither hot nor cold. But, if you pay close attention to it, you can feel the first faint suggestion in the air that this outdoor vigil will finally be a cool one.

We sit in the bleachers at Community Park, here for the second of our thirteen year-old son's four baseball games in five days. His brother's season will begin soon and, of course, our daughter will take to the softball diamond in a few weeks. If baseball is no longer the national religion, there is nevertheless a healthy remnant of believers here in our town. Oh, look! The moon, completely full and bright, is making its appearance, dramatically moving out from behind a wall of mountains directly in front of us. Still low on the horizon, it is turning to pure white as it rises, a wafer for some celestial Eucharist, slowly lifted in offering toward the darkening sky.

I wonder if Teilard de Chardin ever went to baseball games? I suppose his beautiful "Mass on the World" is what makes me see the moon this way. But what do liturgical images have to do with boys playing baseball? Is there a connection between playing and praying? My son is now on deck waiting to bat, and butterflies have begun to flutter in my stomach…. He walked, and was forced out at second to retire the side. And his father's heart begins its return to a business as usual rhythm.

At its best, sport provides an arena in which we may test ourselves and build confidence. The competitive aspect sometimes spoils the whole enterprise, but if we can help each other face challenges, and learn how to lose as well as win, then we will have learned something important. Some athletes talk about the experience of getting into a "zone" in which their whole being—body, mind, spirit—is engaged and they seem to be functioning at their maximum potential almost without effort. All the years of discipline and drudgery finally click in and take over. At that point one is completely focused on the experience itself and not concerned about its instrumental value in relation to other rewards. I would like to be able to pray as well as I breathe, losing conscious awareness of an act that means life or death to my spirit. I would reach the point where praying is not a task, not an instrument, no longer a serious matter. Praying would be like playing and, every now and then, getting into the zone.

One day this week I innocently eavesdropped on an individual praying aloud. I was seated in the reception area of an office and could not help hearing since the door was open. My university colleague's visitor had been preaching to him the necessity of strong steps to convert our students to his particular version of Christianity. His parting shot was to ask his host to join him in a prayer which had the purpose of invoking divine sanction upon all the imperatives raised in his previous remarks. His intention might have been OK, but to me he sounded like a charter member of Bullies for Jesus.

We can be too earnest in our praying, demanding rather than asking. If you really have faith in God you have to take yourself and your issues with a grain of salt. I'll bet God would not mind having a little self-deprecating humor sent up by some of us, at least once in a while. If we knew God well enough, we could do things like that. I'll give it a try.

Lord, I am asking You to pay no attention to these between-the-innings thoughts of mine. The world is a very serious place to be these days, but there are some places that You can ignore from time to time, and this is such a place and such a time. Around here, it is an ordinary Saturday night, the air is clear and cool, and the score is three to two. Amen.

Community Park, Redlands, California, 1979

2. Where Does the Time Go?

My mind is suffering from so many assaults these days that I cannot comprehend any one thing, not to mention having a sense of coherence in my life. As I sit in this restaurant with my coffee, however, I am reminded of one clear fact: today is my sister's birthday. The third of her four children is married now, and she is a grandmother three times over. Was it not just yesterday that she herself chose to be a teen-aged bride? Despite my aversion to cliches, one of the most familiar questions in the English language will not leave me alone today: where does the time go?

A colleague of mine from the university just walked by from several stools down the counter from me with a book in his hand. Seeing me, he stopped to chat. In the process, he recommended that I should read the book, being—so he said—a sensitive person. The title he mentioned is indeed striking: *A Severe Mercy*. If I understood correctly, he described the book as an account written by the surviving partner in a marriage that was terminated by death after a dozen years or so. The title seems to suggest that some spiritual depth was realized through the medium of intense personal suffering. Thinking to ask my colleague a further question just after he stepped away, I turned to look toward the cashier's station only to discover that he had already made a quick exit. The spot where I expected to see him was now occupied by someone just entering the place—a man I do not know personally—but someone I immediately recognized from the cast of several funerals. He is the owner of a local mortuary and a prominent citizen of our town.

So I am beginning to wonder what is going on here! Did I come for a hamburger and a little quiet away from the campus only to be served a triple order of items from some cosmic menu of life's basic dilemmas? I mean, if my sister back in Alabama is getting older in what seems like an awful hurry, what is happening to me? Do I realize the full implications of the fact that time is quietly and quickly consuming the years I have to relate to those I love? Worse still, could it be that I have some severe mercy coming my way? Shall I bitterly conclude that all is not lost even in that case, since the undertaker, at least, will have another customer, make another sale?

No! I will not entertain such cynical thoughts during my lunch hour. But the basic question persists: where does the time go? Christ! I really mean *where*: where is yesterday now? I am beginning to realize that, wherever time goes, it does not vanish. I recall that in the Religion Department of the university earlier this week, we reviewed a master's degree thesis on the subject of the Christian sacraments.

The most remarkable statement the student made in her paper was that our baptism may be a means of grace *when it is remembered*. That is something to think about: a past event as the source of a present blessing.

Dear God! You have secured grace upon grace for us in the storehouse of memory, treasures that wait for reclamation. Since by now You must know how much I would like to be able to pray, I am beginning to suspect that You are teaching me something today. Maybe it is true, as some say, that there is no such thing as a coincidence. Maybe every moment has its message. Maybe there is wisdom in the worn-out phrases we repeat to each other. Time heals all wounds. Experience is the best teacher. Having the time of my life. Time, time, time! O.K., here is what it comes down to. I give You all the time that I have, both my today and my tomorrows. But, most especially, I now trust to Your loving care the whole of my yesterdays. Sift them for the things I really need and give them back to me afresh. My hands and my heart are open, and I am willing to wait.

Bob's Big Boy Restaurant, Redlands, California 1979

3. Are You Security?

It is airports and airplanes again, and doing the usual tricks with my head. I took the Golden West commuter to Los Angeles an hour or so ago and found myself facing a rather healthy walk to the check-in counter for United Airlines. The bags I carried seemed heavier than they should have, and since I was carrying two long garment bags in addition to a bulky piece of luggage and a briefcase, I found it necessary to stop every hundred yards or so and redistribute the load. About half the way along I realized that I was unconsciously shifting the long bag made of translucent plastic in such fashion as to conceal its contents from public view.

Arriving at last at the security checkpoint, I gave the luggage piece by piece to the young woman officiating there and she laid each bag in turn on the belt moving toward the X-ray unit. Through the dimly transparent material, now stretched out face up and flat, she thought she saw something out of the ordinary, turned for a second look, and immediately saw what I had been half-consciously hiding. The black robe alone would not have given me away, but it was the background now for a pure white stole marked at each end by a cross woven of golden thread. In an instant she looked at me: boots, jeans, hair over my collar, mustache drooping downward around the corners of my mouth. She managed another quick glance in the direction the holy cargo went as if to confirm the unlikely prospect of a meaningful connection between it and me. Her response had to be quick; there was neither time nor necessity for talk. What I got was a glorious, made in heaven smile accompanied by gleaming eyes that seemed to say, "Well, all right, brother. All right!"

Gathering the bags on the other side of the barrier, I carefully lifted last the holy one and gently draped it across my back, positioned so that any that looked would see what it contained. The entire load was no longer heavy. Your yoke really is easy, and Your burden is light. Why do I so often think it is too much to carry? Anyway, You were about to drive this lesson home and I needed very much to hear it and take it to heart.

I went on down to the gate assigned my flight and hung the bags on a rack I found there. Secure in my confidence that no one would dare steal them, I set out in search of coffee. As it turned out, this was no small matter: the line at the only restaurant in the area was twenty-five persons long. So I wandered back through the maze of corridors and terminals, up and down through the teeming multitudes of travelers until suddenly I heard an awful cry, "Please come and get me! Don't leave me here!" Well, what can you expect in L.A., I thought, and continued a few steps until the anguished plea was repeated. I turned to look, and some thirty feet behind me I saw a crumpled, aged figure in a wheel chair, her face so distorted by pain and panic that she made an almost gruesome sight. Again she cried out, and I saw that while many, including airport personnel, stared and shrugged their shoulders, none responded.

Then I remembered the stole and the crosses and the smile made in heaven, and I knew I had to go and see what the trouble was. The lady told me that her husband had left her to attend to some matter associated with their travel arrangements and had been gone for an unreasonable duration of time. They were bound for San Diego, she said, but she was unable to tell me which airline they were taking. "Are you Security?" she asked me, adding, "I'm blind; that's why I have to ask." Am I security? Is anybody, really? Are You security, God? There really isn't any security as far as I have been able to tell, but I did not say so to the troubled lady before me. I just assured her that I would not leave her alone and that, together, I was sure we could solve the problem. About that time, a sheepishly smiling little man with a gray beard arrived and the episode, as far as I was concerned, was ended.

I am back now to the immediate reality of departure times, boarding passes, first-class and coach. I am where I am supposed to be and ready to get on with my journey. But in my heart there is another, final intervention. Somewhere deep inside me, a memory awakes and an old country church echoes with singing:

> *I am thine, O Lord, I have heard thy voice,*
> *And it told thy love to me;*
> *How I long to rise in the arms of faith,*
> *And be closer drawn to thee.*

Los Angeles International Airport, 1979

4. Burritos and Burdens

I am oppressed this noon by the complexity of life in a small university and particularly by the pervasive political understanding of human relationships which prevails in it. It is a statement about the human condition, I suppose. There is the ingrained assumption that one gets ahead by ingratiating oneself with those who are susceptible to that tactic, and by putting whatever subtle pressures one can muster upon those who are not. So here I am again, eating alone in a place I know to be seldom visited by university people at lunchtime. The burritos are good here, but they would be better without the burdens I have brought with me.

I am almost late already for a meeting in which the screws will be turned upon me again by folks who feel they are getting shortchanged by decisions I have made. Considerable pressure will be exerted. Facts will be distorted. And I will be cast in the role of culprit. Well, if I accepted the gift of the dog, I should not be surprised to learn that the fleas came with it. It is my part to take what comes, keep my emotional equilibrium, and be as fair as I can be in all my responses. But I can say to myself, at least, that the whole process is excruciatingly painful.

Why have we set things up the way we have? Does human nature in its corporate expressions give us no choice? Christ has called me to place the welfare of others above my own. But *which* others? How am I to judge among competing interests and decide what is best for the institution as a whole? It really does come down to that, however much you rely upon a process everyone has agreed to in calmer times. I am in the judgment seat now. Shall I seek the path of least resistance or do what I think needs to be done and take the consequences? That is a rhetorical question, of course, but it helps to write it down and look at it.

Life, if I am asking You to spare me in difficult circumstances, please ignore my plea. Immerse me instead in the full human reality of life with others and let me surface again a better and wiser person. But is there something I do not yet see that would make a small university a happier place on this side of bankruptcy? So far I have not seen it. Anyway, I cannot sit here any longer. I have to go. In the absence of clear and compelling answers, help me to do my job without losing sight of the really important questions.

Los Jarritos Restaurant, Redlands, California, 1979

5. Stopping the Buck

Since my meeting is not until later in the morning, I have parted from those with whom I car-pooled into Los Angeles and now have an hour or so to kill while they meet with a trustee committee that does not directly concern me. After about fifteen minutes of walking, I have found a coffee shop, come in and sat down. Unfortunately, this coffee shop is located in a huge space where bowling is the principal activity. Since this area of the city is not devoted primarily to retail establishments, I did not have much choice. At ten o'clock in the morning, dozens of senior citizens are setting up a constant clatter as the splattering of pins evokes cheers of delight and collective sighs of disappointment in turn.

Around the elbow of this long counter, a highway patrol officer is doing his paperwork and sipping coffee; his day may be ending as mine begins. Another man reads the morning newspaper while two more engage in a vigorous conversation that is not intelligible from this distance. The other stool-sitter waits impassively for the hotcakes he has requested. Mercifully, the tiny television sets placed at intervals down the length of this counter by Tele-Vend Systems, Inc. are silent so far. A steady chop-chop-chop from the kitchen can be heard when the bowling balls are still. Outside, the traffic noise is dominated by eighteen-wheelers winding their way through this district of warehouses and distribution centers of various kinds.

The human species is about its many tasks: working and playing, hoping and planning, eating and drinking, talking, listening, laughing, learning. And I, what am I about? In the still unaccustomed role of academic affairs administrator I will, moments from now, participate in decisions which will significantly affect a score of lives. More than that, really, if you take into account the fact that the individuals I am referring to have families that depend upon them, emotionally as well as economically. When the wheel of fortune turns for the parent, the child has a lot at stake. Today some, upon my recommendation, will be granted leaves from teaching in order to focus upon research and writing for a year. Others will have their job security confirmed through the granting of tenure. But half a dozen more will have bad news made official: their days of employment at the university will soon be over.

I tell myself that this kind of thing occurs every day; I just happen to be one of the actors in the process at this particular time and place. In a few minutes I will walk down the street to the Bekins Company and sit alone in a conference room to wait for other members of the Personnel Committee to arrive. Since I have been there once before, I know that the room will be dominated by photographs and other memorabilia depicting the history of one of the oldest moving and storage companies in the nation. Faces will look down at me from those walls, faces of persons who in their time made decisions—some good and some bad—for their institution, and it still survives and prospers. I suppose I should find comfort in the presence of those faces, but it will still be a hard morning for me.

I also tell myself that the successful corporate executives and professional people who compose a university board of trustees and its committees are more familiar with this kind of thing than I am and will therefore raise the kind of questions that will keep us from making major mistakes. But, dear God, most of those questions will be directed to me! Although I know someone has to do it, I am still not comfortable with the exercise of power over others. Ironically, I believe that is the primary reason why my colleagues at the university, most of them anyway, want me to do it. They trust me to do what is right for the university and I am trying to honor that trust.

Today I don't have the time to explore what is clearly a philosophical black hole: what is the fairest and wisest way to make decisions in a corporate enterprise of any kind? I know at least this much, that a university, if it is faithful to its mission of discovering and teaching what is true, cannot completely espouse a governance structure derived from business. And an individual decision-maker who is concerned about personal integrity cannot be guided by self-interest alone. My theological training, not to mention my experience, tells me that no one can live in this world and remain completely innocent. One has to muster as much understanding as he can, make a decision and then move on, trusting that whatever mistakes he makes can eventually be redeemed.

Grand Central Bowl Coffee Shop, Los Angeles, 1979

6. Save That Whale!

Although we never said so explicitly, I believe our purpose in coming to San Diego was to say good-bye to the Pacific Ocean. In a few days my son James and I will start across the desert as the vanguard of our family's return to the Southeast. We will go to a new job, a new home, new schools, a new and different chapter in our unfolding life together.

So, in the midst of this hectic time of transition we have tried, foolishly I suppose, to set aside three days for relaxation. One of us, right on the traditional schedule, came down with our familiar vacation virus, complete with fever and other most unpleasant symptoms. We delayed our departure for a day to allow him to get rid of it, which he did, apparently by passing it along to me. Where the virus went we did not know until we arrived in San Diego. But, again, that is the usual pattern.

Right now we are passing some lazy moments in this vast and beautiful Mission Bay Park. The day is heavily overcast, with clouds from horizon to horizon, and a constant, chilly wind makes us wish for jackets. But we do not complain. All of us love such a day, and each in turn has mentioned that it reminds him or her of Alabama. It is a foretaste of fall days in the South, which are drawing nigh at a pace that is hard for us to comprehend. It often seems that the critical decisions in my life are *given*; once the reality of the change begins to set in, I find it hard to recall the details of whatever rational processes led to the decisive moment. I think this results from the biblical notion of the call: when you hear *that* voice you just get up and go. That is the way I understand what is happening to us now, but the transition is tense and difficult anyway.

Does it make sense to sit on a park bench in this secular paradise and think of some far away sacred magnet tugging at my mind and soul and body? Do other people feel this way sometimes? I certainly do not think of myself as being singled out in a way that others are not. But the idea of being called was central to the religious culture in which I grew up and it continues to be a significant influence in my life. While I reject any notion of divine election to special office or status, there is an awful lot in the Bible about people being asked to take responsibility for specific tasks. I suspect that any person who faithfully listens can hear such callings. Among the biblical characters, Jonah suddenly springs to mind, bringing with him a note of comic relief.

Just a few miles across the corner of this bay is a place called Sea World. Given the direction of my thoughts for the last few minutes, I should quickly say a special prayer. Dear Lord, do not trouble Shamu, that trained and ready whale! Save him for someone even more reluctant than I am. As for me and my family, we will arise and go to Atlanta, that great and wicked city.

Mission Bay Park, San Diego, 1979

III.

Out of Europe

In our last year at the University of Redlands, my wife and I suddenly had the opportunity to travel to Europe for the first time. A faculty member who was to accompany a large group of students on a travel study trip, visiting England and France before arriving in Austria where they would spend the rest of the semester, decided rather late in the game that he could not go. It was felt that I, in what turned out to be a brief tenure as head of academic affairs, should go with the students to familiarize myself with what had been for over twenty years one of the most popular programs of the university. And there were administrative matters to be negotiated with the on-site staff in Salzburg that could best be handled by me directly. Further, once we accompanied the students to Salzburg and dealt with our business there, we were invited to make brief stops in Rome and Athens, destinations to which the students would travel later in the term. I felt the call of duty and agreed that we would assume this unexpected burden of responsibility!

This will seem like a diversion, but the point will emerge rather quickly. My parents grew up in rural Alabama in the early part of the twentieth century. Their childhood homes were unpainted and without electricity or plumbing. Cooking a meal first required that one build a wood fire in an iron stove, and the only source of heat in the rest of the house was an open fireplace. To my knowledge none of my grandparents ever had what you would call a job. They were subsistence farmers, which meant that virtually everything they ate they raised, hunted and killed, gathered from the wild, or bartered for. It was a task that required the labor of all persons in the household and there were more persons in the house than is typical today. There were eight children in my father's family and seven in my mother's. Graduating from high school was not the norm for them and their peers although some made it and a few went to college.

What I am getting around to is relevant to my first encounter with Europe. As far as I have ever been able to determine, my family has no awareness whatever of its ancestral roots. Over the years I have asked a number of older relatives about this. I feel fortunate even to know the name of one of my great grandparents; beyond that there is very little that I have been able to learn about any of them from their descendants. It is said that my paternal great grandfather "came from Georgia." That's it. One of these days, perhaps, I will do some genealogical research. But my point is that, whereas people like me are commonly referred to these days as *European* Americans, we have never thought of ourselves in that way. *Never.* Beyond the loose observation that we came from Georgia, we have had little curiosity about our roots. No doubt there are historians who know, but the question of how all these poor people came to populate the rural South, scratching out survival from the dirt, is not one I have a ready answer for.

I suppose our story could be written as another tale of victimization, but that would not interest me at all. There is more than one kind of poverty and I believe that the generation before mine remembers childhood as a rich experience, and—in their own lives—they have done well. Most migrated to the cities to get jobs or were called up to spend a period of their lives in military service. They experienced the Great Depression, World War II and the period of prosperity that followed. Most of their children went to college. In my case I have often quipped that once my parents got me to college I decided to stay. And I have a cousin who has been elected and re-elected to the U.S. Senate. It is fair to say that I come from a line of people who are honest, hard-working, decent and proud to be Americans. For the most part, they feel that life has been good to them. But our sense of where we came from reaches only to the rural, southern part of the United States.

For me to go to Europe was not like Alex Haley going to Africa. I have enough education to recognize the dominant European and African influences in the culture of the South, but I do not feel the personal connection to another land that many African Americans do. My first encounter with Europe was profound to be sure, but as I prayed around the edges of those experiences it was the whole human story that I encountered rather than some particular version of it. Obviously, my perception of things, and the way I interpret them are conditioned by the fact that I am indeed a child of western civilization in general, and of western Christianity in particular. But the desire to make meaning of history and human experience, both to celebrate its glories and to lament its atrocities, is a universal instinct, common to all who have enough food, freedom and time to think things over.

To visit Europe for the first time is to see a lot of castles and cathedrals. These are often splendid testimonies to the aspirations of the human spirit. But there is no escaping the evidence of the darker side of history, the bitter story of our sinful inclination to have power over our neighbors and sacrifice their lives to satisfy our greed. We are endowed with a great capacity both to create and to appreciate the beautiful. We sing, we dance, we make music, art and architecture. We are capable of, and often show great compassion for others, even to the point of surrendering our own lives for the greater good. In more than equal measure we have plotted against each other, cheated, lied, raped, pillaged and murdered; and we have rather frequently done these things under the banner of some noble cause. An encounter with history will throw both dimensions of human nature right into your face. And, when you think globally, there is only one thing more perplexing than this encounter, and that is the realization that the basic situation has not changed.

The forms of Christian spirituality with which I am most familiar find ways to bracket out the reality of universal complicity in the propagation of evil. I am prepared to admit that this may be necessary to some degree in order to avoid madness. One makes no contribution to human welfare by being morose. But I cannot be satisfied with a faith that assures me that *my* sins are forgiven and implies that all the world needs is more people like me. There is an awful, inescapable, moral ambiguity at the heart of personal existence. Innocence is not an option for anyone but children and they lose it soon enough. My quest is for a spirituality that takes history and human experience seriously. I want to pray with my eyes open. At the same time I do believe that the experience of delight is indispensable to our spiritual well-being. We are born to laugh as well as to weep. And we have an appetite for beauty that must be fed if the human species is to survive.

While I do not wish to veer too far into theological reflection, what I have said so far reminds me of how indebted I am to the thought of the Protestant Reformation and to the seeds of it planted by St. Augustine and St. Paul. Christian faith is not one thing or the other; it is one thing *and* the other, essentially paradoxical. We are simultaneously right and wrong, lost and found, saved and damned. If we do not understand this it is because it cannot be understood. It can only be lived. Perhaps this perspective makes me a European-American after all. At least this is the way, many years after the fact, I interpret the private thoughts I hastily wrote here and there as my wife and I served as neophyte shepherds for thirty-three college students on our first trip to Europe. To these prayers I have added two written several years later.

1. Let the Light Win

Our third day in Europe and I am still suffering from the modern malady of jet lag. I am tired all day, but my body refuses to acknowledge that night is night and will not sleep. Even the darkness is as light to thee, my poor body! (*Psalms* 139:12)

Darkness and light is the theme of this day's experiences, and perhaps of the entire trip so far. This afternoon, we have seized the opportunity to pursue our private agenda apart from the larger group and have found our way to the Tate Gallery. We are here now amid the collected paintings of J.M.W. Turner, one of our primary targets during the brief stay in London. Turner concerned himself with the interplay of light and shadow as a constant theme in his work, often with a great deal more shadow than light. But the light is there, mysterious and beautiful.

Here in this temple to the human imagination, my mind keeps flashing back to yesterday, to the tour of the Tower of London, that ancient complex of prisons within prisons. The Tower is an overwhelming testament to the shadow side of human nature. There we heard the stories and saw the implements of cruelty, torture and death. The hideous axe leaned in repose against the chopping block where human beings knelt as if to pray. Visible on the block were the scars left by the violent downswings of the axe which, having severed a human head, spent its remaining force against the block itself to leave a series of now horribly eloquent depressions in the silent wood.

It should be noted, though, that the axe was reserved for victims of high status who were allowed the special privilege of being beheaded in relative privacy. The rest were hanged in the public squares and parks, to a chorus of derisive jeers from the mass of fellow human beings. God! Did You know that things like this were likely to happen? I am sorry to say so but, right now, Your own public execution doesn't seem enough to set the record straight. I understand the theology, and it all works out rather neatly that way. But the reality! What a vicious sword we have made of the cross itself!

But somehow we do not give up. They say that Turner was enthralled by the destructive forces of nature: storms at sea and consuming fires on land. But the light in Turner's paintings grew brighter and brighter as he grew older, at last becoming a glorious blaze which obliterated virtually all form and structure. Whether the artist would consent to it or not, I want to see in his work the triumph of the light. If You gave us the option of violence and death, which we have explored to the utmost, You also gave us a receptivity to the Light. Don't let the darkness win! Let the Light shine and let us all see it together.

The Tate Gallery, London, 1979

2. What the Stones Say

How lucky we are tonight! This place is a palace compared to the little hotel in Bath last night. It was an iceberg, and some of the students have sore throats in addition to being bone-weary. So we are all glad that our accommodations tonight are not only sumptuous, but also quite warm.

Directly across the fields outside our window, Salisbury Cathedral rises in its majestic splendor, a glorious sight indeed with its graceful spire ascending more than four hundred feet. Piercing the night sky, its silent stones compose the most eloquent of prayers. And so we come to the close of a day that has spoken much about the human propensity to pray.

We began this morning with a frigid walk around the plain on which the massive boulders of Stonehinge maintain their sturdy circle against the winds of winter and the devastation of time. It is said that this arrangement of stones was a calendar of some sort that let the people know the times for planting and other vital activities. But they also served a more directly religious purpose, perhaps as a temple for the worship of the moon. Even today spiritual descendants of the ancient Druids gather at the place once a year for a ritual observance of some kind.

Does it matter whether one prays to the moon or the god we call God? Probably not, just as long as one prays with integrity. Does it matter whether one prays at all? Maybe not, if one agrees that a lot that passes for prayer isn't, and a lot that doesn't, is. Is it too much of a cliche to think of true prayer as an attitude of the soul, needing neither formal address nor verbal content? I love many of the corporate prayers of the church, but sitting here this evening the words will not come, unless perhaps these words, right here on this page, are also part of the great silent chorus that pours from the hearts of the faithful, from generation to generation.

For the most part I just listen and look, trying to hear deeper echoes in ordinary conversations and to see beneath the surface of commonplace things. Sometimes I think I hear another voice and see another face in the crowd, and I am aware of a Presence I cannot explain. Perhaps it is the voice of Everyman I hear, a whisper of what is universal among us and within us.

It is too simple to say so, of course, but Stonehinge looked toward heaven for a long time before we sent Salisbury soaring into the same sky. I don't know if You prefer one to the other, or if You have ever been impressed by either. But the *people* who raised all these stones in Your direction, Lord; the people. I know You are moved by the people in all their groping and striving. You must be moved by the people!

Rose and Crown Hotel, Salisbury, England, 1979

3. To Show an Affirming Flame

This morning we attended Matins at St. Paul's Cathedral in London and sat directly under the massive dome designed by Sir Christopher Wren. The pure notes of the boys' choir lingered as the sounds lifted, assuming ethereal after-tones in the vast space above us. The cathedral *works*, convinces one that eternity intersects time in its chambers and transports the human spirit for a brief moment into the presence of the Source from which it came, and to which it aspires to return.

St. Paul's Cathedral stands on a hill that has hosted holy places for many centuries. The first structure here may not have been Christian at all, but a temple erected for the veneration of the goddess Diana. But the first Christian church on the site was in place as early as the seventh century. It is jarring to learn that houses of worship on this hill have been destroyed time after time by fires, by Viking raiders, and most recently by Nazi bombs during the second World War when the cathedral was severely damaged. And yet St. Paul's still stands on the hill in all its storied splendor.

We experienced St. Paul's as tourists always do, including the obligatory walk around the circumference of the magnificent dome. And yes, we stood in the designated places and whispered our greetings to our comrades across the chasm. Our muted voices were indeed audible from one side of the circle to the other as promised. But I am glad our group chose to do more; we returned early this Sunday morning to answer the invitation of this holy space to raise our hearts and our voices in praise to God.

I was somewhat startled by the way the service picked up themes which had been in my awareness all week. The Old Testament lesson was from the first chapter of the book of Genesis, God's spirit brooding over the primitive chaos and taking the risk of creativity. In the beginning the Creator brought light into interaction with darkness and the endless cycle of evenings and mornings was underway. Soon God made man and woman in his own image. Reams have been written about what it means to say that we are made in the *image* of God, but I like most of all the suggestion of Dorothy Sayers that it means we are creatures endowed with the capacity for imagination. God set us down in the midst of the darkness and the light to see what we would do with the gift of freedom. One thing we did was to imagine glorious cathedrals and build them, complete with windows that celebrate the splendors of light. The other thing we did was to fig-ure out ever more ingenious ways to destroy both them and ourselves.

The New Testament reading was from the first chapter of *The Gospel According to John*. It says that given the choice between the darkness and the light we seem to prefer the former. But it also says that the light still shines, bringing new possibilities in the wake of every calamity. The sermon we heard was simple and straightforward: sometimes we have confidence in life and sometimes we do not. What really counts is the basic outlook we maintain in both good times and bad. Faith is seeing life as it really is and saying *yes* from the depths of one's being. It is an affirmation that—although one sees the darkness with all its injustice and terror—one chooses to trust the light. A faith that hides from the dark realities of history and personal experience is not faith at all since it arises from a basic *no* to existence as it really is.

I have remembered more than the preacher said; his words touched the core of my spiritual conflicts. The horrors of this world did not stop when St. Paul's survived the relentless bombing of London. But it is not the major catastrophes alone that feed my doubts; it is also the suffering of the innocent little ones that continues in every time and place. The creation is badly out of joint; there is no way for a truly honest person to deny this reality. And yet, the Light still shines in the darkness. And I find that I can still say the Yes and still trust that the Light will somehow win. My prayer today draws a phrase from W.H. Auden that has meant so much to me for so long. Dear God, you know how hard it is for me to see the world as it is and still hold my head up. There is just too much mindless violence and suffering, and we seem so powerless to make things better. Nevertheless, I ask You, please help me, every single day, to "show an affirming flame."

Bus from London to Canterbury, 1979

4. The First Lamp of Evening

We have crossed into the German countryside where a fine snow has powdered the open fields and forest floors. The thin mantle of white is just sufficient to accentuate the roads and rooftops, the stumps and stones, the cars and trucks to a degree that is magnetic to the eye and a stimulus to the imagination. The old-style trains we pass in the station yards, the appearance of the German language on signs, and the resemblance between the caps worn by the trainmen to those of the Nazi era combine to evoke an eerie recollection of the events of World War II. My consciousness of those days is largely through films, and through whatever impressions the newsreels and papers made on my mind as a child. The presence of the snowy fields beyond the tracks also brings forward powerful images of war from the film version of Boris Pasternak's *Dr. Zhivago*.

But something about the winter landscape suggests calmness and quiet rather than war. The snow scenes of Monet and Sisley in the Paris museums come back and once again evoke that sense of a mysterious silence settling down upon the Earth. It is a benign silence which shields the human spirit from the cacophonous uproar of modern life and allows one the opportunity to hear what speech might arise from his own depths.

Perhaps it isn't a voice at all that one needs to hear, but the sound of the stillness itself. There is too much of thinking and talking, too much of planning and calculating, too much of worry and anticipation. So, in these few moments, I will simply pause and receive the stillness. Outside the train window dusk begins to fall, mingling with the mists already present, and the first lights appear in the villages. So come, holy quietness, I am waiting. Descend like the mist covering these lovely meadows. And, in some window of my watchful soul, even now, the first lamp of evening appears.

Train from Paris to Salzburg, 1979

5. The Geography of the Soul

As the sights and sounds of contemporary Athens begin to find their special place in the storehouse of memory, my spirit is lulled by the harmonious murmuring of the DC-10's mammoth engines. Far below us the frozen landscape just within the Arctic Circle, barren and white, looks up at us without so much as a hint of hospitality.

If contemporary Athens assaults the senses with its bewildering barrage of visual clutter and the constant discordant chorus of honking vehicles, the land below presents the opposite extreme. There are only stark shades of white, utter stillness, and—one assumes—very little in the way of sound save, perhaps, the howling of the wind. And yet the mind is unsatisfied to label such a place barren. There is a geography of the human spirit that corresponds to the diverse regions of the physical world. I know there is a downtown Athens in my soul, but not so much of it as in many people I know. And as I get older I find I need to spend more time exploring the uncharted realms of stillness within me.

The soul's barren places beckon us from time to time, and it is essential to surmount the initial sense of threat as one moves tentatively away from the familiar traffic of normal routines. I do not mean that I must take myself to another place; I mean that I must find a different place in myself, and go there not to take action, but to wait and listen, even for the faintest stirring of the wind across the unobstructed plains.

Flight from Copenhagen to Seattle, 1979

6. But Who's Counting?

This morning, on a train from London to Gatwick Airport, my seat was located in the midst of an extended family. As best I could tell, the entourage was escorting to Gatwick a pair of grandparents who were on their way to Texas. There were about six or seven persons, all of them British and all apparently kin to each other. A little girl about five or six years old sat facing me, with her grandmother in the adjacent seat. There were others in the seat behind them and two women facing each other directly across the aisle from me.

The little girl was quite a chatterer and very fluent with her sentences, most of which were questions. I was more than usually interested because during two weeks in England, I had not had direct contact with small children. So I listened raptly to the girl's voice, somewhat nasal in tone, lilting in its cadences and, of course, distinctly British in its accents. A boy, the girl's slightly younger brother, came around to stand in the aisle in order to be nearer to the middle of things. As adults will do, they combined talking to the children about the grandparents' journey with questions of an educational or entertainment sort. "How many twenty-fives in a hundred? How many fifties?" Some time went by before I realized that I, a stranger who had smiled, but not spoken to the party, had become part of the children's audience. The girl had been performing for me with all her talk, and she was aware that she had won my interest and approval. This became abundantly clear when the drift of things took a sudden sharp turn against her.

"What do four fifties make?" asked one of the women across the aisle, whom I assumed to be the children's mother. Like a sudden bolt out of the blue, the answer came from the boy standing in the aisle silently until now. "Two hundred!" he suddenly exclaimed, catching his sister off-guard and seizing center stage. "You should know that," said the mom to the girl. "Your brother knew it straight away. What do six fifties make?" Two little minds churned quietly for a moment, and when the girl's correct answer came, the moment was immediately spoiled by an adult's response. "You're counting on your fingers still? You shouldn't be doing that anymore."

The little girl immediately burst into tears—not sobs, just tears—and turned around to bury her face in the back of the seat. Beginning to repair the damage, Grandma said, "But she is good with her writing. She already knows how to make proper sentences." And, after a brief pause, she patted the still faceless girl, adding softly, "You're really all right, you know." Slowly, and by tentative degrees, the child turned around to rejoin the circle, balling up a moist facial tissue in her hands and blinking against the light to restore her spoiled vision.

When the episode seemed closed and her little brother returned to the spot in the aisle he had abandoned in the crisis, she leaned over toward him and, in a soft, secretive voice, asked, "What is half of one million?" "Five million!" the erstwhile genius promptly replied. "No! It's five *thousand,*" came the sister's hissing retort, with a slight elevation of her shoulder to show superiority. Turning aside, she closed the exchange with a facial expression that seemed to say, "Now we both know you are actually quite stupid." And, yet again, the entire story of the human condition had been retold.

Gatwick Airport, London, England, 1984

7. A Singing Revolution

It is my sixth and final night in Estonia, a small country I never imagined I would visit. Just minutes before midnight the sky is still blue and a chorus of frogs is singing in the nearby woods. This hotel is located in a residential neighborhood on the outskirts of the ancient city of Tartu, and we are within walking distance of a Baptist seminary which, like this hotel, is of recent construction, via a path through the neighborhood and a small forest. From the front yard of the seminary's only building, you can see a vast complex of high-rise residential buildings constructed during the Soviet occupation and now quite run-down in appearance, much like many public housing projects in major American cities. I am here with a few other American guests for the annual European University Chaplains Conference, attracted not least of all by the great Tartu University, founded in 1632.

Although the first written reference to the city of Tartu is from the eleventh century, excavations have shown that human beings built fortifications on the hill behind the university hundreds of years earlier. Indeed, a stone altar from ancient times still sits in a circle of stones on the site today. Mock sacrifices are still offered from time to time as medical students burn their notes on the rock following final examinations.

What I am taking away with me tomorrow is the strong impression of a people still holding their heads up in spite of hundreds of years of domination by foreign powers, most recently the Soviet Union. Lying in the path of the Nazi invasion of Russia in the second world war, the Baltic states were ruled by first one and then the other as the tides of war shifted back and forth. Under Nazi dominance, hundreds of thousands of Jews living in the area were killed. When the war ended, the Soviets established firm control with as many as 60,000 Estonians being deported to Siberia or killed. This was followed by decades of Soviet occupation and suppression of Estonian culture, a period only recently ended. A young woman who met with us during our conference remembers being forced to sing, in Russian, songs that glorified Lenin. "I did not even understand the words," she said, "but we had to sing them."

A week ago, I flew with two American colleagues to Helsinki, then took a ferry across the Strait of Finland to reach Tallinn, the capital city of Estonia. With a couple of hours to kill before continuing our journey southward by bus, we asked a taxi driver to give us a quick tour of the city. He was eager to do so and since he was Russian himself and did not speak English, he confidently expected that we would understand if he spoke in German. We did understand this much, as he stopped beside a large park, speaking and gesturing with great excitement: that very night one hundred thousand people would gather as one massive choir to sing Estonian songs. It has become an annual celebration of freedom and cultural pride. Later we learned that, as Soviet power and resolve weakened in the eighties, the Estonian people began to sing their own songs more and more boldly. Such was the power of this gesture that the departure of the Soviet army in 1988 is referred to as "the singing revolution."

Oh, the power of songs! No matter how sophisticated my education and experiences have allowed me to become, I can now confess without reservation that it is the singing of hymns that has made me who I am. This is not to say that I am an orthodox believer or even that I have compelling answers to the most urgent questions that life continually throws at any thinking person. But one Easter Sunday in my youth our closing hymn was "Take the Name of Jesus with You," and somehow I thought it was a summons intended for me, and I have never been able to forget it.

The Estonian people have a very long legacy of suffering at the hands of foreign powers, as do so many others. But nevertheless they still gather to sing their songs today. People of African descent have been through hell in America, forced to leave their homes against their will and become the personal property of other human beings. But somehow they have sung their way through it. We must, all of us, keep singing no matter what happens. May God bless the Estonian people! May God bless us all.

Ihaste Hotell in Tartu, Estonia, 1998

IV.

South Toward Home

In a vocational sense, it has so far been my good fortune to recognize when the end of a chapter in my life story is approaching. More fortunate still, every time of transition has ended with the emergence of a new challenge and a new chapter in my life. I know this is not true for everyone, not even for most of us in this land where there is so much freedom to change course and move on to the next thing. Some just never get into the educational process sufficiently to qualify for good jobs. Others earn good wages for a time only to have their jobs eliminated through technological innovation. Some go to the best schools, enter businesses and professions where they have money and status, marry and have children, buy homes and cars and boats, and still have the inner core of their lives disintegrate for a variety of reasons. I have been fortunate indeed. My formal education has prepared me for life as well as work, and my jobs have kept food on the table while also feeding my need to invest my time and energy in meaningful and help-ful tasks.

Which is not to say that I have always been happy at work. I would match my miserable days with anyone else's. Many times I have been driven to the edge of the abyss emotionally, caught between a rock and a hard place by the conflicting demands of people and institutional circumstances. One of the chief ironies of my life is that my uneasiness in the limelight somehow lands me in leadership roles. I have to assume that my reticence inspires trust. For example, when I was interviewed for the chaplaincy post at Redlands, I was asked why I would be will-ing to give up the position I had at the time which carried with it tenured status in the faculty. My reply was that tenure meant nothing to me because I under-stood myself to be a chaplain rather than a professor. The chair of the search committee later told me that my answer to the question was one of the key fac-tors in the decision to hire me; it showed that, unlike some others, I would not use the chaplaincy as a way to get my foot in the door of the faculty. Nevertheless, in three years I was chair of the Religion Department (in addition to the chaplaincy) and in six I was the acting Vice President for Academic Affairs. But my primary calling remained intact: I got right back into the university chaplaincy when the opportunity presented itself.

At this time in my life I can take the long view, and when I do so, it is clear to me that, all things considered, life has been very kind to me so far. We all wonder as the years go by what our lives would have been like if we had made different decisions early on, and I am no exception. I am grateful and glad that I have occasionally been called away from my primary role as a minister in higher education to do something else. And I wonder from time to time what my life would have been like if I had stayed in academic administration or teaching when the opportunities were there. But the following reflections, like those that preceded them, are not really about my particular vocational journey. It would be wrong for a reader to think that one has to be an ordained minister, or be theologically trained, to have the kinds of experiences I have described. I think Thomas Merton had it right when he said

> ...there is only one vocation. Whether you teach or live in the
> cloister or nurse the sick, whether you are in religion or out of
> it, married or single, no matter who you are or what you are...
> you are called to a deep interior life, perhaps even to mystical
> prayer, and to pass the fruits of your contemplation on to others.

What I am trying to say is that my professional life, as fortunate as it has been, is not what I am writing about. I am writing about my interior life and, in doing so, inviting others to a new awareness of their own life experience and how they have processed it inside themselves.

The California years stand out as a really special time for me and for my family. But even though lifelong friendships were made and life, in general, was good for all of us, that chapter, too, had to come to a close. We missed sudden showers of rain and autumn leaves. We needed to be closer to family and the deep South was still home for all of us but our youngest who actually knew her native Alabama primarily as a place she had visited. The chance to go to the dynamic city of Atlanta and, for me, to work as chaplain in a university with several professional schools, including a seminary, was a new challenge. In this case the chair of the search committee told me after the interview that the job would be offered, and he advised me not to take it! It would not be long before I understood what he meant, but I remain glad that I took the job anyway and kept it for a little over a decade, drinking deeply of the bitter as well as the sweet.

What follows are random moments in the life of a particular university chaplain. It is not an attempt to talk about important themes such as the role of religion in higher education. And the selections do not all reflect the principal challenges in my life during the years in question. Again I say that this is not an autobiography in the usual sense of the word: the systematic re-creation of a life story told chronologically. But it is about vocation in the sense that all of us wonder about the meaning of what we do from day to day. It is a topic I have continually thought about, but only occasionally put into writing. I begin with an evening during the early days when I was in Atlanta without my family.

1. She Touched Me

Tonight I am learning a new, deep lesson on the importance of relationships with other people. I have lived alone in a new place for only about eight days. But my wife of twenty-one years is on the opposite side of this continent in California, waiting until the house sells before she can join me here in Georgia. We do not know when that will be. Tonight I thought a better than average dinner might cheer me up, but as I sit and wait for sautéed shrimp I have already begun to pour my feelings out, writing all over a paper place mat.

You have to have family and friends if you are to keep your soul intact in this world. It doesn't have to be a traditional family, just a circle of folks who care deeply about us, and we about them. So, dear God, hear me. If ever I have inwardly complained about the burdens of parenthood; if I have entertained a false and foolish fantasy about the carefree life of single persons; if I have regretted the necessity of daily toil that others in addition to myself may eat and be clothed; dear Lord, forgive me! I know, *how* I know in this moment, that I cannot be myself by myself. I know You have made me, and each one of us, for others, for life in relationships. And I have those relationships in great abundance, beautiful, holy, loving relationships: wife, sons, daughter, brother, sister, mother, father, friends tried and true. And, although I may feel a bit isolated right now, I am profoundly aware of all these ties to others and I am grateful indeed.

So now comes the further thought: let me be for all these dear ones what they are for me. Open me still further to their needs for support and affirmation. And beyond the circles of intimacy that are especially important to me, open me more and more to those dear strangers who, no less than myself, stand in need of love and care. In this new city and new job, lead me to those persons I am best prepared to help. And, above all, grant me this further wish: that in finding myself in and for others, I may be found again by You.

I managed to stop writing long enough to finish my meal and it was quite special, even if unshared. Then this happened: I asked the waitress where I might find a certain store and she quickly told me how to get there. As she turned to leave, she gently placed her hand on my shoulder; not just a touch but a gentle grasp that seemed to say, "I'm lonely too, sometimes." I almost thanked her for reaching out to me that way, but the verbal acknowledgement would have robbed the gesture of its power. She must know I got the message. I hope she also knows how gratefully I received it.

Jim White's Half-Shell Restaurant, Decatur, Georgia, 1979

2. Evening Lamps

Our flight has lifted from the runway at Birmingham and we are twelve thousand feet above the ground, a third of the way up to our cruising altitude toward Los Angeles. Below us in the twilight, and stretching to the horizon, is a puffy, soft floor of blue-gray clouds. The sunset has left at the rim where sky and horizon meet a brilliant swath of red and orange, the last linear blaze of this day's light. Wisps of cloud above the glowing perimeter are catching the receding light now and giving the sun one final chance to prolong the day. Since I cannot see directly to the west, I must be missing a still more spectacular sight. But what I can see is enough to send an old hymn from my youth rising from that fondly remembered past:

> *Day is dying in the West,*
> *Heaven is touching earth with rest;*
> *Wait and worship while the night*
> *Sets her evening lamps alight*
> *Through all the sky.*

How I love that sentiment. I *will* wait! I *will* worship! I will watch for the heavenly lamps of evening and in my heart I will sing this hymn of gladness. But I ask you now, dear Heaven, would you mind touching with rest not just earth in general, but one earthling specifically? I am talking about *me*. Light some lamps in the dark and empty chambers of my soul this night and I will, by their soft illumination, find my way through this difficult time of transition.

I am not really making this special request for myself, but for someone I love more than I love life. These days are terribly difficult for her and I am going home now to try to help her with the final details of leaving the house we have shared with our children for the last seven years. The moving van has come and gone. When I get to Redlands it will just be a matter of us all getting into the car and beginning the long drive to Atlanta. The change is not easy for any of us, but my beloved seems to have sunk her roots a little deeper than the rest of us have. She loves our home, the town, and our circle of dear friends. And her work with the elderly has built relationships that are especially important to her. If I could just be calm and strong, and if there could be some new light in my eyes, somehow radiating reassurance, things would be a lot better for her, I know. Light an evening lamp or two for me. For us.

United Airlines, Birmingham to Los Angeles, 1979

3. A Real Breakfast

What a surprise to find right here in Emory village such a mellow eating establishment! It is half Georgia country and half laid-back California funky. The coffee comes in ancient white ceramic mugs and, by golly, you get real cream to put
in it. You sit in plain old wooden, slat-backed chairs and nobody seems to care if
the place, well, needs a bit of maintenance.

Whatever might be said about the physical appearance of this place, the waitresses supply the finishing touch to the overall ambience. They are wearing ker-
chiefs on their heads, deliberately old and nappy sweaters, faded jeans or
gingham, ankle-length, well-worn, un-pressed skirts. There is an unmistakable
suggestion here that, at Ed Greene's restaurant, at least, the counter culture I left
in California is alive and well in the shadow of Emory University. True to form,
one waitress with long, braided hair escaping her black, back-knotted kerchief
takes advantage of a lull in the action to sit at a table and pluck her breakfast, kernel by kernel, from the heart of a cracked-open, ruby-red pomegranate.

The only appropriate thing to say to all this would have to be *right on!* A
poster on the paint-thirsty wall says, "You don't fear non-air…unwater…? Are
you slap out of your lasting plastic tree?" Tell it! This place is real. The waitresses
are real; the customers are real. And somewhere back there in the kitchen, I'll bet
you, Ed Greene himself is real. The world is real today and I am real, too. I want
to jump up and say, "This is the day the Lord has made; let us rejoice and be glad
in it! Hooray, all right and amen!" I feel at home in Atlanta already.

Ed Greene's Restaurant, Atlanta, 1979

4. Let the Stillness Stay

I should not be here. It is 9:00 a.m. and I should be in my office crashing to meet the deadlines that will rise up to greet me the moment I walk through that door. I wish we did not place such a premium on busy-ness, but it is ingrained in the American psyche. Like almost everyone I know, I have an internal program that requires some kind of certifiable accomplishment on a regular basis. I am busy, therefore I am. But now and then we take on so much that the energy and attention circuits overload and not enough gets done. Then those dreadful twins, frustration and fatigue, come to visit.

It is by such a path that I have come to be sitting here in the university cafeteria and basically staring at the pastry and coffee on the table before me. Why give my body a sugary snack when it is my soul that needs to be fed? Somehow I hope that, in the space of a few minutes, I can find a little stillness and quiet at the center of myself before moving on to the day's demands. How I wish that the Stillness would not only come, but stay with me as a constant companion! Even now, as I reflect and write on the napkin I have unfolded before me, the Stillness draws near and stands on the boundary of awareness. Oh, do come in, please! Come right in, my dear friend. How very welcome You are on this Friday morning. Sit with me for just a few minutes and let me show you some of this week's pictures from the scrapbook of my mind.

Here is One, a graduating senior, finishing college with a heavy debt, not knowing what the immediate future holds, having no firm ideas about vocation, struggling yet with the expectations of parents who have placed their hopes in him, worked hard to see him through this place. He doesn't know what all this means, how he can be who he is, find his own meaning and still be their fulfillment, their pride. As he finishes the dinner of higher education he realizes that he has never been bold enough to look at the menu.

Here is Two, who has just lost her mother to a terrible disease. She is struggling but strong, teaching us, her spiritual guides, how one copes, keeps one's head erect when times are really tough. And here is Three, who has found it necessary to break a long-standing relationship with someone she still loves very much. I agree that it was something she had to do. Only after hearing her story did I really know the meaning of Jesus' hard saying, "If your eye offends you, pluck it out." She had to excise an important part of her life, else both she and he would be cast into yet undetermined hells.

Oh, holy Stillness! Help me today if You please. Help these students, my friends, find You; these and many others like them. Visit them with Your great gift of serenity. If that is not possible, if they cannot or will not answer Your call because they are too busy and too preoccupied with their problems, then stay with me today and let me show You around this place. There are many others here You need to meet. A university is not an enchanted island floating securely off the coast of the real world, believe me. For all our good intentions and hopes, this campus, any campus, has an unquiet heart. So some of us must come to the outer gates of academe and beg You to come in. Stay for a while this time. For at least this one day, go where I go. Just stay with me.

Cox Hall, Emory University, Atlanta, 1981

5. Getting A Golden Mouth

Now here is an unlikely place for reflection. I have been sitting for what seems like forever in the clinic provided by the Emory Dental School. I do not mean that I am in a chair in the waiting room. For more than two hours, I have been in a chair reserved for persons whose teeth are being repaired by students in training to become dentists. There is no way I could rightfully be called a wimp because I am a seasoned veteran of dental care provided by students. At Loma Linda University in southern California I allowed a student to use a tooth of mine to perform his very first root canal. I will never forget, as the novocaine took hold, listening to the professor tell my student how to use that collection of little files. That one root canal took several appointments to complete, each lasting around three hours. But the finished product, presided over by a professor of dentistry at every step of the way, was excellent in every respect.

So here I am again. We are today in the process of finally seating four dental crowns in my mouth, two made of gold and two of porcelain. Right now the latter two have been taken back to the lab for a final application of heat which will finish them with the proper glaze. My student dentist sits beside me now, polishing away on the gold while we wait for the porcelain to bake. He will graduate in a couple of weeks and then join the Air Force to repay Uncle Sam for financing his professional education. His formal education will be completed, but this conscientious young man will continue to learn and grow for years to come.

It has been my good fortune to be involved in the educational process virtually all of my life but, fortunately, it has not always been in the role of guinea pig. To tell the truth, though, I guess you could say that many people along the way have taken risks by allowing me to learn how to be a chaplain by trusting me to help them. And I am sure that my own professional education has not been entirely free of pain for those in my care. I know it has often been painful for me! Every sermon I have ever prepared has been extracted from my mind and heart with considerable anxiety—no doubts about that! It occurs to me that there was a man in the early history of the church who was so eloquent that he was nicknamed "golden mouth" (John *Chrysostom*). Maybe if I get enough gold crowns on my teeth I will be a better preacher and not have to work so hard at the task!

My student has gone back to the lab and will return soon to start placing the new hardware in my mouth. The professor has checked it all out and says we are ready to go. I am grateful for whatever contributions I have made to the education of several young dentists. And I am thankful for the opportunity to receive excellent dental care at bargain prices. As for the pain, well, what I have endured—here and elsewhere—is minimal indeed when compared to the lot of so many of God's children in this world. Why so many must suffer is something I will never understand. I can only pray to be a more significant part of the healing than I have been so far.

Emory University School of Dentistry, Atlanta, 1986

6. What We Are, Who We Are

Visiting the laboratories where first year medical students dissect human bodies continues to be a profound experience, shaping my understanding of what ministry is or, better, what a profession is. Today I stood in the hall outside the anatomy lab talking with a student. We were soon joined by others to form a small circle of conversation. The first student told me that the emotional impact of radically cutting and probing into a human body did not really hit him until the dissection of the face, an act that finally removed the last vestige of identity from the person lying on the table. He said that he had thought a lot about the fact that what he had done would, in any other setting, be an outrageous and criminal act. What is it, he wondered, about a small group of persons on an admissions committee that allows them to grant permission to do what he is doing in that room behind us? There seems to be a very narrow line between the authorization to do such a thing and its otherwise reprehensible character. Having had this experience, he said, it is hard to imagine that someone could then decide not to become a physician and simply walk away and do something else.

This occasion provided me the opportunity to tell the students that the word "profession" is religious in its origins and that the dissection of the cadaver could be understood as an initiation rite into something akin to a monastic order. Once you pass through the initiation ritual it is difficult ever to return to the "outside." I pointed out to him that the same is true in other traditional professions such as the clergy. Another student said that when he went home over the Thanksgiving break his friends all responded to him in a new way, treating him as though he were already a doctor. Another said that during the first week in his new apartment, even before attending his first class, his landlady had told all his neighbors that "a young doctor" would be living in the building. All of these remarks confirm the experience of being set apart from others as soon as we enter the long road toward certain professions.

This is a problem with which I am very familiar. When, in high school, I accepted "the call" to be an ordained minister, I was immediately set apart as *different*. It was reported to me that one of my peers, upon hearing the news of my decision, replied, "What a pity!" On the other hand there was instant high esteem from many. Years later I was to read that entering the ordained ministry is like putting on a "self-acting suit of armor; so easy to put on, so difficult ever to take off again" and I knew exactly what the author meant. This is such a complex issue that I wonder if it can be understood by anyone who has not experienced it from the inside. I have to take *what* I am seriously because it enables me to do a lot of good. But I cannot let what I am completely define *who* I am; and the reverse is also true.

I am trying to help the medical students recognize this primary ambiguity and tension between professional and personal identities. I do not want my doctors to break into tears when they give me bad news, but I do want them to care. Each of us has to live with the tension between who we are and what we do. If that tension goes away completely, the result is uniformly dismal: you get either arrogance or incompetence in a physician, lawyer, pastor or whatever. Going to medical school can be a brutalizing experience, making you want to insulate yourself emotionally. I suspect that the same is true in other professions, but perhaps less dramatically. The really wonderful thing about being a university chaplain is that you have more freedom to be yourself as you do what you do. I am learning from these medical students as they are learning from me. It doesn't get any better than this, and dear God, I am profoundly grateful for this experience.

Cox Hall, Emory University, Atlanta, 1986

V.

A Pilgrim on Peachtree Street

When I was a child growing up in Birmingham, Alabama, we thought of places like Memphis, New Orleans, and Atlanta as peers with whom our city competed. This was especially true of Atlanta, the closest of the cities to us. It was baseball that made us aware of this rivalry. In the Southern League, the Atlanta Crackers were the team we most wanted to see the Birmingham Barons beat. It was especially nice when this happened at our own Rickwood Field. But, overall, the competition between the two cities had ended by the time I graduated from college. By virtually all measures of urban progress, Atlanta had surged ahead. Given the more notorious aspects of its history, it is easy to put Birmingham down, but that is not my intent here. The simple fact, as everyone knows, is that Atlanta made the decisions it needed to make to become what it is today, a great international city.

This is not to argue that Birmingham is a second rate city. Given the choice of a place to live now, many would quickly choose my hometown over traffic-clogged Atlanta. I would make that choice myself. But the situation was very different when I graduated from Birmingham-Southern College in 1959 and enrolled in Atlanta's Candler School of Theology at Emory University. The seminary at that time was not a very exciting place, but the city was coming to life in dynamic ways. I thought Ralph McGill's column in the *Atlanta Constitution* was truly prophetic and I raced to get the paper every morning to see what he would say. And I loved the way Mayor William B. Hartsfield dealt with the Ku Klux Klan. Once he responded to their threat of a massive rally in the city by saying something like, "Come on, boys. We will be ready and we will bang your heads together if you do not behave yourselves." Given the leadership of these two and many others, Atlanta soon declared itself to be "a city too busy to hate."

What I am saying is that the city of Atlanta influenced the course of my young adulthood significantly. It presented itself as a "new South" just as it had after the

Civil War, and that made it an exciting place to study theology and otherwise prepare for a lifetime of ministry. During those years it was my great good fortune to participate in a group composed of students from all the city's seminaries, including the historically black schools. While it was still an officially segregated society, our interracial group met in homes on both sides of the city, including—on at least one occasion—the home of Dr. Martin Luther King, Jr. When I graduated from theological school I went back to Birmingham and stayed there for 10 years. But through all those years, the Atlanta of 1959-62 remained an important influence in my life. And although I knew that the place had changed dramatically over the twenty years since I left, when the opportunity to return to Atlanta came, I took it.

In the preceding section I shared some of the private moments of reflection that occurred during my years as University Chaplain at Emory. Like the whole collection presented in this volume, those pieces do not focus upon the big events and major personal struggles of those years. I have never been a disciplined writer even when it comes to recording private thoughts in a personal journal, and I have been least likely to write in times of crisis or when under the greatest pressure from daily tasks. So I have tended to write only when, by circumstance or choice, I have broken away from the main business of life and work. But I did discover that my fascination with Atlanta tended to focus on its best-known thoroughfare, Peachtree Street. Given the slightest opportunity I would break away and go there just to walk, ride, look and listen. If any street in America merits the metaphor *artery*, it is this one. Peachtree Street begins in the heart of Atlanta and throbs with urban vitality and excitement for several miles to the north. Still loving Atlanta in general and Peachtree Street in particular, I continue to go there every time I have the opportunity.

1. Brother Juniper Calls My Name

Today I have officially begun my long-anticipated pilgrimage on Peachtree Street. I suppose the rain is what finally made me get up and give it a try. A gray and overcast morning has a way of closing in on one and turning the process of thought in an inward direction. And when a gentle rain like this one sets up its own soft symphony, the day takes on peculiar qualities of sound as well as sight. It was settled early: I would take the next few hours to seek confirmation of the notion that, if I walked along this special street as though it were a tributary of the river of life itself, it would tell me some of its secrets.

When I first came to Atlanta twenty-one years ago to enroll as a theological student in one of its several seminaries, Ponce de Leon Avenue was the route we took to go anyplace at all. We simply stayed on Ponce until we got to Peachtree, then turned left or right depending upon where we wanted to go, unless our destination was the Fox Theater, in which case we were already there. This morning I reverted to that old pattern, turned left when I got to the Fox and made my way downtown, successfully negotiating all the Y intersections which were so confusing at first. I drove slowly past Central City Park, its fountain gushing superfluously in the rainy air.

Beyond the park, things were less familiar to me and I slowed down as much as the press of traffic would allow. I passed the massive concrete edifice over the Five Points rapid rail station, the apparently defunct Miami Bar, Abe's Furniture store and a whole block or two of businesses largely unfamiliar to me. According to the street map I studied before leaving home, Peachtree Street should begin abruptly just beyond this area. I soon confirmed that, traveling south, the signs begin to say Whitehall after you cross Memorial Drive, even though the map shows Peachtree stopping, or starting, a few blocks before. I drove maybe a quarter of a mile on Whitehall, turned around, and started slowly back toward the origin of Peachtree Street. This would be it, the start of my peculiar pilgrimage, and all of my senses went on full alert.

When Sir Launfal mounted a fine horse and dashed gallantly from his castle to begin his search for the Holy Grail, the first sight to greet him was a poor beggar seated at his gate. Crestfallen, Launfal cast some coins at the unfortunate man's feet and forged ahead. While the goal of my journey is considerably more modest than his, I too was not prepared for the initial spectacle on the way. The first structure I encountered on Peachtree Street was a jail! A modern brick building with sinister slits for windows, it is the new "Pre-Trial Detention Center" of the city of Atlanta. Although I had read about its opening a few months ago, I did not know exactly where it was. Now I am confronted by the reality that this jail sits at the gate to Peachtree Street. The visual impact is worsened by the fact that the new jail is surrounded by the garish facades of bail bond offices.

The mystical mood was shattered, at least for the moment. I circled around the block, parked the car and, confused, approached the jail on foot. There were lovely flowers at the door, but once you are in the small chaste lobby, you have to speak through a circular hole in a thick, glass barrier if you have anything to say and, apparently, I didn't. I hung around for a few minutes and decided that, while I must deal with the spiritual significance of this turn of events if my journey is to have integrity, I did not have to do it today.

Back in the car, I convinced myself that what I really needed was breakfast. Stopping for breakfast is one of the better moments in a journey by car, and what would be wrong, on this first day, with just making a little survey of the street to note likely places for return engagements? Drifting along, I remembered a restaurant called Brother Juniper's that I had never visited, but should have. It is operated by a religious community to which, I have heard, one of my former students belongs. So I moved deliberately again, back past the Fox and First Baptist Church, making my way to Midtown.

I have been sitting at a table in Brother Juniper's for some time now, long enough to finish a wonderful breakfast, linger over coffee, begin to think and, for about an hour, to write. I had, believe it or not, something called "The Parson's Plate": eggs scrambled with cheese, ham and scallions; whole-wheat biscuits and home-fried potatoes. There is much to like about this place in addition to the food. The ambience, all wood and warm colors, seashells and other natural objects, reminds me of small cafes operated by young people around San Francisco during the era of the counter culture. But, most importantly, this is a place where they ask you your name when you order and when your meal has been prepared, they call for you. It is a very nice touch. "Don, your breakfast is ready!"

I have been on this urban journey for only a few hours and already I have found an establishment where they call you by name. They have just called Helen. Before her, it was Bob. Suddenly I think of the nameless men and women I saw just moments ago, lined up outside St. Luke's Episcopal Church, waiting for the only daily bread they are likely to receive. And here I sit, well fed indeed, and savoring a blessing almost as welcome as the food: someone called my name.

Now what shall I say about this pilgrimage which is barely underway? Have I found a sign telling me either to continue or to stop? Has Peachtree Street called my name? If not, why have the goose bumps now come out in full force? There is a Presence is in this place. Is the soul of the city drawing near? Is the great nameless Namer of all somewhere on these premises? I think so. Oh yes, I do think so. Now comes the wonderful surge of gratitude that is the essence of prayer. How profoundly glad I am in this moment to be one human being among the multitudes that comprise this marvelous city!

What I want to do, what I really want to do now, is to go out onto Peachtree Street and begin to call the names. Maria! Mike! Tamika! Ahmad! Old man poking through the dumpster for aluminum cans! Old lady with your bulging, battered, shopping bags! Fresh young jogger flush with promise, bursting with life and hope! Listen! I am calling each of you by name and I am announcing that there is a table prepared for you. Oh someday, somewhere, I know there is a table prepared for you. For all of us together.

Brother Juniper's Restaurant, Atlanta, 1980

2. Is That Nod for God?

This morning I am a little bit off the principal avenue of my pilgrimage, but not by much. I was ambling toward the federal building to see what is going on there, but found I could not pass the Hot Cookie Corner on the ground floor of Rich's Store for Homes. So I am sitting here against the windows, having finished two fresh oatmeal cookies, and nursing a second cup of coffee.

It is a gray and gusty morning, but the early rain has stopped. I see the people coming and going along the sidewalks and many of them see me, perched here like an animated mannequin programmed to scribble on a yellow pad. As I look toward Forsyth Street the buildings, framed by the window beside me, are a pastiche of gray, brown, beige, white and black. But from this angle one of them stands out. First Federal Savings has *bronze* windows and an odd shape to it. The only way I know how to describe its design is to say that it appears vaguely edible. The basic support structures, rounded, smooth and horizontally stacked, seem to have been pushed into symmetry by pressure from above, an architectural confection where the icing has oozed out from beneath each floor. That thing wasn't built; it was baked!

Here in this place there are few customers, few that is who stop to sit down with their cookies. Since the Hot Cookie Corner is open to the larger store, most come from various stations inside and return from whence they came, taking their purchases with them. But one young man has attracted my attention. He sits facing away from his table in order to converse with the women behind the counter. I cannot understand what he is saying, but I note that his body is moving from the waist up, gently but steadily rocking back and forth as he speaks.

It occurs to me that there are two possible explanations for this young man in motion. In novels I have read that there is a characteristic nodding response which heroin addicts affect when they are high. It could be that my fellow patron down the way is under the influence of that dreadful drug, but I seriously doubt it. On the other hand, that rocking motion is also associated with a form of prayer, most characteristically the prayers of devout Jews at the temple wall in Jerusalem. I have no other reason to assume that the young man is Jewish and I figure it unlikely that the language of his body arises from motives which are devotional in origin.

But the latter explanation is nevertheless the one I prefer to imagine. I want to understand the Hot Cookie Corner as an appropriate place to pray. Prayer is an impulse to recognize the dimension of the holy in the most commonplace situations. The idea that some places are holy and other places are not holy makes sense, but it does not go far enough. In holy places the dimension of depth and inwardness is highly focused, forcing the mind to acknowledge its presence. But a secular place need not be seen as an unholy place or even as a spiritually neutral zone. It is rather an environment in which the holy depth is hidden. If one enters such a place for no good reason, and if he lingers there in a mood of watching and waiting, the holy Presence will peek out from behind whatever hides it from view. But I must leave here quickly to avert a possible misunderstanding. Involuntarily, my body has begun to sway.

The Hot Cookie Corner, Atlanta, 1983

3. Facing the Inequitable

It is lunch break time at the "Interdisciplinary Conference on Capital Punishment" being held at Georgia State University. After hearing a very logical defense of the death penalty, I have eaten a meal, which I hope will not be my last, and have now taken my place in a downtown park among many others. They are using as much of their lunch hour as possible to bask in the springtime sun. Some of us sit in a small amphitheater whose stage is presently opened up to accommodate an assortment of pools and flowing waterfalls—a clever design. The sounds would be as pleasant as the sight were it not for the presence of a young man with a barely portable radio who obviously feels that the act of carrying such a load to this spot demands a comparable return of energy in the form of volume. Ah! He is walking away. As the soulful sounds recede in the distance, the relief to the ears is stunning. And the crowd has begun to disperse, leaving the place to the pigeons and me.

To my left, just across Peachtree Street, a modern building rises, at least thirty-five stories high, which is black in color. Even the windows are so tinted as to appear quite dark. I am struck by the observation that, across the very top of this edifice, in huge white letters, stands the single word, EQUITABLE. What an important word it is. It obviously brings to mind again the comment of this morning's address, that equality and justice are two separate things. The speaker was making the point that, if the death penalty is applied unequally to blacks and whites, this does not prove the case that capital punishment itself is unjust. His claim was that, on these grounds, the evidence argues not for the abolition of the extreme penalty, but rather for its equal application. But, as I see the matter, to be treated equally is not necessarily to be treated justly. Two individuals may be equally abused.

Not far from this spot a few months ago, a young black man picked, at random, a young white woman walking along the sidewalk on a crowded downtown street and fatally shot her as she passed. He then killed himself, administering his own death penalty. Dear God! Was the score thereby made even? My heart cries out for that gentle woman suddenly struck down, murdered on her birthday. Murdered! But my heart is not helped by the thought of reciprocity, a life for a life, however it came to pass. What confusion of mind, what anguish of spirit, led that young man to enact such a senseless double tragedy?

Lord, You have not set things up in such a fashion as to insure an equitable world. Things could be improved in the future if we all try harder to make the world a better, safer place. But at this point there is no way that we can balance the scales of justice in human history; they have dipped down way too far in the direction of horror and suffering, wrong heaped upon wrong, to ever be made straight. I think the plan is for You to do it on the last day if I understand what the Holy Bible says about these things. I have to trust some version or other of that scheme in order not to go mad. But I am finding it unusually difficult today.

For myself, I just wish I could be better, could make more of a difference. Can we, by killing, reduce killing? I wish I knew. There is no way I can claim to be a pacifist, for I know there are situations in which I would kill, or condone killing, in an attempt to prevent a greater atrocity. There are situations, too many of them actually, in which one must act in the absence of moral certainty. In creating the world, is that what You did? Did You think it was worth it to take the risk that things would turn out as, in fact, they have turned out? Are You really in this with us? After a lifetime of church going, I know the available answers. But some days the questions just will not be turned aside. This is one of those days.

Central City Park, Atlanta, 1980

4. Lighting Up Atlanta

The invitation was irresistible. Come downtown on a certain Friday night and dance in the middle of Peachtree Street in the heart of the city, it said; we will light up Atlanta for you. So the people came into the city to have a party in the street. Lots of us. That it was going to be a big party became evident as soon as we set foot on the MARTA train out in DeKalb County. Hundreds poured in at every stop and none got off.

As we got packed closer and closer together, I found myself face to face with a man for whom the party had apparently begun several days before. I looked at him and he looked at me; there was really no alternative under the circumstances. Struggling to remain erect, the man leaned even further toward me and announced, "I am a drill sergeant. A drill sergeant in the United States Army!" Although I harbored private doubts about the claim, it seemed the part of prudence not to give them voice. Instead I said, "That's good," or something equally innocuous.

The sergeant studied me intently for a long minute and finally asked, "You know John Wayne?" It so happened that my admiration for the late movie hero vastly improved in the space of about three seconds, and we were able to agree that John Wayne was indeed a *man*. He was a drill sergeant's drill sergeant, no doubt about it. Seeing that we agreed so heartily on the really basic matters, we rather ceremoniously shook hands. Not once, not twice, but *often*. The train by then bursting at the seams with human cargo arrived at the Five Points station just as my reluctance to describe my personal record of heroism in combat was becoming a problem.

Once on the street we saw that people were streaming in from every direction: all sorts of people; young and old; prosperous and poor; all colors and shapes and sizes. They came until it was almost impossible to move, not to mention dance, in Peachtree Street. They came until there were 300,000 human beings pressed together between the tall buildings on a short segment of the pavement and parallel sidewalks. Many came simply to see; others came, less simply, to be seen. Some had rented hotel rooms or found perches along the perimeters of parking decks in order to watch from a safe distance. More than a few scaled power poles where they could both see and be seen simultaneously. It was in many ways a terrible spot to be in. In the midst of the throng one had a strong sense of being at risk, in mortal danger even. At the same time, there was a sort of mysterious power present, something larger than the sum of all of us together.

It was indeed a celebration of the city. We purged this famous street of its customary business and claimed the priority of flesh and blood over concrete and steel. When the climactic moment came for fireworks to burst into the night from the top of the Georgia Pacific building, we stood, all 300,000 of us, shoulder to shoulder, and looked expectantly toward the sky. It was as though we had come together to say to some celestial observer, "This is who we are and this is what we have done—we have raised up a splendid city with magnificent buildings and now we are posing with them. Look at us!" Yes, there is extraordinary power in the act of gathering. Let everyone come to the party! Fill the air with music and decorate the nocturnal sky with bright streams and bursts of brilliant color! And for the sake of the city, let us dance the night away.

Peachtree Street, Atlanta, 1984

5. Body Language for the Soul

Why is it that places that were significant for you long ago always seem smaller when you return after an absence of many years? As I sit in the empty nave of All Saints Episcopal Church, my initial pleasure upon finding the place open is giving way to puzzlement. I remember this church as being much larger but, of course, it was not. The bare wooden floor and pews without cushions also surprise me, but without disappointment. It is better for the music this way and, besides, it is the gathered people who give a church its warmth.

But why do I not remember these remarkable stained-glass windows? More than anything else it is the windows that grasp me today and I want to understand why. Predictably, they tell the story of Jesus Christ from the angel's first visit to Mary to the cross and resurrection of her son. But the overall mood is somber and introspective, with various shades of blue and purple as the principal colors. I have walked around the room just now looking at each window in turn, but I am drawn back to the right rear corner.

Here is a forlorn presentation of Jesus as a young adult. The brighter portrayal across the room of the precocious child in the temple, astonishing the elders with his questions, is a distant memory now. Almost lost in this corner is the isolated prophet-to-be, feeling the weight of his future. In the desert by himself, he senses that he is utterly alone, spiritually even more than geographically. The austere landscape shares his desolation, and his white garment absorbs the deep purple of the distant hills, accentuating the downward droop of his head and hands. A lone black bird drifts in the heavy sky and, in the lower left-hand corner, a serpent slithers toward the darkness.

It is odd how the position of the fading sun in this window seems too high to be compatible with the nearness of the night. I take this to mean that the descending dark is in the inner life of the young man God has chosen to bear the whole weight of the world's infidelity and sin. Why do I find this the most authentic of all the windows here? Is it because, when I was last in this place I was a young man myself, and in a state of confusion about what God was getting me into? Perhaps. But I am here today to remember and be grateful for a very small gesture, more than twenty years ago, which began to let the light come in again for me.

I came here twice when I was a seminary student at Emory University, came just because I was curious about Episcopalian worship. Since I was in a state of intellectual revolt against the doctrines of the Christian church, I do not know why I supposed, if I did, that I would find anything appealing in a traditional liturgy. Curiously, the thing that impressed me the most was the observation that as the cross was borne down the aisle in the processional, people bowed as it passed the pew where they were standing to sing the hymn. To this day I do not fully understand why, in that moment, I said to myself that I wanted to visit this church again so that, when the cross passed by my pew, I too would bow. I did come back, and I did bow when the cross passed by, and in the act of bending my body something broke loose in my soul, and I have never been quite the same since that moment.

I did not know at the time that the bow is among the most profound of religious gestures. I did not know that in addition to expressing gratitude, the bow has a peculiar capacity to produce it. I did not know that day that simply tilting my head forward and bending ever so slightly from my waist would open a floodgate of feelings inside me, with the dominant sensation being that this place, this company, these Christian people, belong to me and I to them. Way down deep I knew that all my doubts and fears and reservations and resentments would not change that fundamental fact of belonging. From that moment I began at last to reaffirm my religious identity and calling, but I never came back to this place again until today.

There is indeed a language of the body. But it is not merely the case that our bodies help us to communicate with others. Our bodies help us to communicate with ourselves as well. If I want to experience gratitude but the emotion will not come, perhaps it is because I am literally not in a position to receive it. Today I want to express my appreciation to this church for its unassuming witness to me so long ago. So I will get up quietly now and stand once more before the young and lonely Jesus in the window. And, in this Thursday silence, I will bow.

All Saints Episcopal Church, Atlanta, 1986

6. Some Monkey Business

Here in this commercial paradise known as Lenox Square, throngs of us are in the final stages of countdown to Christmas. Actually, for my part, things are in pretty good shape. I am here right on schedule, two days before the holiday, doing the last bits of low pressure purchasing that I always hold back as an excuse to mingle alone in the holiday crowds.

I was somewhat startled just moments ago to come upon a group gathered around an old-fashioned organ grinder and monkey. Children and adults alike held out coins which the smaller primate accepted, pocketed, and offered a tip of his cap as a gesture of gratitude. If you stood and watched for longer than a few minutes, which I did, the surprise and delight soon gave way to uneasiness. "Willie the monkey" was working very hard, virtually in perpetual motion, and the signs of fatigue were apparent. But after a few more minutes Willie removed his cap entirely and turned to face his master. The organ grinder explained to us that the gesture was a prearranged signal of fatigue and the desire for a break, then opened the door to a small cage beneath the organ and Willie went in for a few moments of relaxation and privacy.

My first impulse had been to accuse the man of exploitation, but this agreement which had been worked out between the two of them confused the situation. Perhaps, together, they have just found a way to make ends meet; perhaps, between the two of them, it isn't as bad a life as it might otherwise be. Certainly for millions of the species *homo sapiens* today things are much worse.

Now, with a cup of rich coffee before me I have positioned myself in a place that allows me to indulge my passion for people watching. For several minutes I have had in my field of view a middle-aged man wearing a coat that is unmistakably mink. I am not talking about a long coat; this one is cut in the fashion of a World War II flight jacket that stops abruptly at the waist. I believe these are called Eisenhower jackets, but they are not usually made of mink. To top off the image, the luxurious dark collar has been carefully raised from the shoulders to caress the back of the man's neck. This furry embrace, blending with his own dark hair, accentuates the circle of white that is the bald spot on the back of his head. Oh well, one can't have everything, and anyway this man with blue jeans below and fur above still has pizzazz. Just seeing him here in this crowd makes me happier still. His clothes proclaim, "I am here and I am who I am." Well, OK then, I say. OK!

I hate commercialism, but I love Lenox Square. I love it even when it is jammed with people in a do or die shopping frenzy right before Christmas.

Maybe I am attached to the place because when I first came here, during my student days at Emory, it was brand new, a dazzlingly modern environment for stores. My wife would be quick to point out that shopping is not on the list of activities I enjoy, and she would be completely correct. What I like is watching the people in a crowded place and being one of them at the same time. Our materialism is awful and it corrupts the season. But at least in all this buying today we are thinking of other people and buying gifts for them rather than ourselves.

Still, our way of Christmas is shot through with ambiguity. I love the variety of images on the cards we send, from very traditional pictures of camel-riding wise men following the star to abstract impressions of birds and trees. I especially go for scenes of snowy villages in New England with their horse-drawn sleighs and smoke curling upward from farmhouse chimneys. But I also think about the dark side of the season to be jolly: folks getting drunk and driving cars into telephone poles and into each other. And I am painfully aware that the way we celebrate the birth of Jesus exerts enormous pressures on fractured families and relationships. A friend of mine has told me recently that he doubts his ability to make it through another Christmas. He is not alone in feeling so low as the blessed day approaches.

Then there is the accelerating problem of the disparity between the haves and the have-nots. Sitting here and watching the crowds go by, laden with stunningly wrapped gifts for their fortunate families and friends, one can get the impression that the have-nots are few. But it isn't so. Dear God, it isn't so. And I have to acknowledge that my often haphazard attempts to be Your servant have earned me a place among the haves. Exactly what to do about this state of affairs is not clear to me. But I don't intend to sit around and mope during these holy, happy days.

At least I have not lost the capacity to hope for Your coming. At least I remember the story of Your birth among us, and of Your identification with the lonely, the lost, and the forgotten. And I also remember that You went to wedding feasts, talked a lot about banquets and even used a pun or two when you spoke. I believe You laughed a lot; I hope so anyway. I am glad You have freed me to live joyfully amid the contradictions while trying to do my part to make things better. So when I see Willie the monkey collecting pennies for his master until his fingers are raw, I am still able to long for the time when the lion will lie down with the lamb, and reconciliation will cover Your whole creation like the morning dew.

Lenox Square, Atlanta, 1979

VI.

Plane Songs

If there are personal characteristics that define the core majority of Americans, one of them has to be our impatience. You know you are a typical American if you have ever stood in a supermarket check-out line designated "Fifteen Items or Fewer" and counted the items in the basket of the person ahead of you. We do not like to wait. When television sets were first in our homes, we had to wait briefly for them to warm up. This was seen as such a problem that a way was found to keep them "warmed up" while they are turned off. Now days we turn them on and they snap awake instantly. Progress! We can eat breakfast, withdraw money from a bank, make phone calls, and leave our dirty laundry to be cleaned without getting out of our cars. Having to wait can quickly make most of us angry and some of us fly into rage.

High technology is increasingly programmed for our homes as well as our cars and workplaces. Work is actually being done on a kind of bar code device one can wear which will store information about you such as, for example, what kind of music you prefer. When you get home from work and enter your home, the music you enjoy will begin playing automatically, lights will come on and so forth. We want to be efficient. A man wrote a book telling us seven ways to be "highly effective" and it became a runaway best seller. I am not sure just what it means to be an effective person. One who gets the most out of the adage, "time is money"? We are incurably impatient. We want to know the quickest route to any destination or goal, the way that requires the least investment of time.

Well, I do not know how it happened, but somehow I was endowed with the gift of patience. I *like* to wait. When a supermarket cashier apologized to me for a momentary mechanical delay of some sort, and I told her not to worry because I enjoyed waiting, her face flushed in response to what she could only interpret as an insult. In my mature years, I have come to love gardening. You have the seeds for a while, then the sprouts, then the stalk, then the blossoms, then the tiny tomatoes and still you have a long way to go until the harvest. Outside of some powerful fertilizers and some fail-safe genetic work to make the plants resistant to disease and certain insects, there is really no way to speed up the process. The waiting is half the fun.

Since my work involves extensive travel, I spend a fair portion of my life in airplanes and occasionally dealing with unanticipated delays: a flight is canceled or held back indefinitely due to a fog in Atlanta or a thunderstorm over Dallas. On such occasions, some people get red in the face, assert the importance of their mission, demand that the gate agent find a way to remedy the situation, and even threaten to sue. I have heard them do this many times. Other people have brought along books for just such a development and appear to read contentedly while some, God forbid, allow themselves to be sucked into a stupor by the omnipresent airport television channel. Not me. I see the sudden necessity to wait as an open door to God knows what. I will quickly enter that door and walk through the entire airport if there is time, and my mind will be totally engaged in the related activities of looking and listening. I anticipate that I will see or hear something that will surprise me, and I usually do.

More of my private prayers have come to awareness in airports and airplanes than in any other place. I believe this is true not only because I spend so much time in such venues but also because the coming together of so many people on so many different errands is exciting in itself. There is also the mystique of being able to travel so far so fast. Of course, the romance of travel disappears after about four or five trips when you are traveling on business. It is a brutal process these days, battering the spirit as well as the body. But that is all the more reason to bring along your imagination when you have to get up and go. The human scene is alive with messages and meanings for those who are spiritually awake and alert.

1. City of Angels Down Below

It is always comforting to know that you have successfully made the connection from one flight to another in a major airport. One little hop through the air and I will be close, at least, to home. I love this twenty-minute flight from Los Angeles International to the regional airport in Ontario, California. This time it should be quite special: the air is clear and I anticipate seeing this vast city in the moments when dusk is turning to darkness. By the time we are up, it will actually be more night than day. How marvelous it always is to savor the twilight transition from one to the other!

I love planes and I love cities. This little commuter seats only sixteen persons, and I am sitting five feet from the open door of the cockpit—close enough to read the instrument panel. Now the two engines obey the pilot's summons to test themselves by giving back a throaty roar that causes the little craft to shudder in response. And we begin to move to our appointed place on the maze of runways, showing appropriate deference to the giant airships coming and going, to and from all parts of this precious globe.

It is our turn to go now. The small turbo-props bore invisible channels through the thick evening air and draw us forward faster and faster. We're up and climbing higher and higher. Quickly, the Pacific Ocean appears beneath us, then banking sharply to the left, we turn to face the vista I had hoped to see: a vast and sparkling Los Angeles, itself an ocean of lights. The freeways are flowing arteries of red and white bubbles; the major boulevards appear golden-hued with their sodium vapor lamps; and ordinary white bulbs mark the innumerable smaller streets, row after row like some luminous cotton crop now ready for harvest.

Lord, is it true that you spend your time in rural places, that you are far more comfortable with trees and mountains than with tall buildings? I ask you what is more beautiful than Los Angeles in this mood, seen from this angle? Oh, I know: up close it can be, and is at this moment, quite ugly and filled with pain. I do not forget all your children down there right now, from Hollywood and Beverly Hills to Watts and the barrios of East L.A. How we all need You, need something, need somebody to bring us together as one nation, if not one family!

But we have left the city sky now, and surrounded by all the dark spaces the lone freeway below looks like a shimmering serpent, twisting and turning to attack the city from the east. Dear God! Call the snake away from our urban places! Give us another chance to do things right. Or just go ahead and send down that new city you talk about at the end of Your book. I don't know how much longer we can wait.

Well, we are going down to San Bernardino County now and I am ready to call it a day. Have You been reading over my shoulder, watching me scribble these words on a Golden West barf bag? It's not Hebrew and it's not parchment. But it is the best I can do tonight.

Golden West Airlines, 1979

2. It Will Be Now

On this trip I have been reading Carl Sagan's *Dragons of Eden*. He takes a hard-line view when it comes to the nature of human beings, saying that we are completely physical phenomena. There is no dualism of flesh and spirit of the sort implied when we speak as though our minds are not totally dependent upon our brains. Whatever "mind" may be, it is completely a function of the brain. "What is man that Thou art mindful of him?" Sagan would answer the Psalmist's question by saying that Man is that animal whose brain is largest in relation to the mass of its body, and whose neurological system is most highly developed. That, and nothing more.

Still, Sagan seems to savor myths such as the Garden of Eden story. He thinks these ancient stories may reflect a kind of genetic memory. The myth of Adam and Eve, for example, may represent a dim recollection of the time when the breakthrough to knowledge of good and evil did indeed become a conscious reality. And there was a point at which individuals became aware that death is their inevitable destiny. Although the garden story is best understood as a picturesque metaphor, aspects of it may be literally true. There was a time when snakes did not have to squirm along on their bellies and childbirth did indeed become painful only with the dramatic enlargement of the human head (knowledge).

If we are not the traditional composite of soul and body, our physical existence nevertheless bears the stamp of a memory which reaches back all the way to the origin of life. If, as Sagan believes, all creation began from one cosmic event, the mystery of eternity may be somehow encoded in our brains.

The pilot says that all those hundreds of light spots on the Texas earth beneath us are the sites of oil wells. Does his interjected comment interrupt or extend my encounter with Sagan's science? Those vast pools of energy hidden beneath the crust of Texas are themselves the residue of the very ancient past. And it is odd to consider that this modern airplane, screaming across the sky, is powered by the organic remains of prehistoric plants and animals. There is an analogy here to Sagan's point. All the experience of the living past is stored in the deep recesses of our minds, waiting to be discovered.

What a coincidence it now seems that, when I first buckled myself into this seat, I scanned an article about memory in the airline's magazine. It advanced a limited version of Sagan's surmise about genetic memory, claiming only that all our individual life experiences are stored in the deepest caverns of our minds, waiting to be reclaimed, refined, and put to use. And now we have the oil wells beneath us. Maybe those wells provide the strong metaphor I need to bring all these thoughts together. Is there a way to tap into the rich pools of memory buried in our brains? What sort of wells would we sink, and where are the prospectors of the human spirit who can say just where and how we might begin our search?

Meditation may be one tool that can burrow deeply enough into the seams of stored experience to strike the crucial connections between our present and our past. Is our memory really so much deeper than we suppose, carrying within it the vestigial remains of the whole process of creation and evolution as well as our own childhood experiences? Can we in fact gain access to the stored experiences of the entire human race?

Suddenly now, I want to stop all this thinking and just sit back quietly and wait for whatever notions may volunteer themselves. Streaking through these smog-screened skies, physically powered by the organic legacy of the eons, I acknowledge the spiritual wisdom of all the ages past. I break through the crust of conventional assumptions. I open all the seams and channels I can reach. I welcome the pouring forth of a profound sense of connection to my Mother Earth and all her children. I am where I am supposed to be. I am here now. Yes, I say. Yes.

What time will it be when we get to New Orleans, my seatmate asks. It will be *now* when we get to New Orleans I want to say. It will always be now.

Delta Airlines over Texas, 1978

3. Will You Know Him?

A mother, who looked too young to have a ten-year old son, stood with him and her own mother at a suburban airline ticket counter. There being only one employee present, I took a seat nearby to wait my turn. Reservations were being made to send the boy to see his father who, apparently, had been separated from the family for a significant space of time. "And how old are you?" the smiling lady behind the counter asked the boy, who was wearing toy sunglasses with radiant neon green frames. "I'm ten!" he exclaimed, clearly proud to have moved into double digits. But as soon as the words were out, his demeanor abruptly changed and he hastily retracted them. "No! I'm nine! I meant to say I'm nine!" he insisted, and he looked up at his mother for her response to this departure from a script which had clearly been rehearsed. If this has something to do with his eligibility for a discount fare, I thought, she will secretly nudge him somehow. She did so, with a playfully extended toe against his leg.

Being unable to ask for his driver's license in any case, the gracious agent smiled and said, "You must be having a birthday real soon." "That's right," he said, "I'm having a birthday real soon." He beamed up at his mother, both of them sensing relief, but they were not entirely successful in repressing their need to giggle. Embarrassed, but nevertheless in on the conspiracy, the grandmother sought to move the conversation on to safer ground by interjecting, "I think you two have your tickle boxes turned over."

The agent went on to point out that age ten was the cut-off point for certain regulations governing the care of children traveling alone. (It never became clear if a fare decrease was also involved.) Through age nine, a flight attendant must insure that the child is met by an appropriate person when departing the plane. At age ten and beyond it is assumed that the child is old enough to know better than to leave the gate with a stranger. "Will you know your father when you see him?" the grandmother asks. "Sure I will. It hasn't been *that* long." But the poignancy of the question hung in the air, and it is all I can remember about the closure of this scene. There had to be the "Have a nice trip" finale, but I could not hear anything after that question.

Given the prevalence of divorce in our society, it is not hard to imagine the skies over America filled with children bound for summer reunions with one or the other parent. The single parent family is commonplace now days; perhaps it is the experience of most of our children. But the question grates against my sense of how things ought to be, and it will go on haunting me for a while longer, the question with its deep spiritual nuances: will you recognize your father when you see him?

Eastern Airlines ticket counter, Decatur, Georgia 1990

4. To Save My Life

Three flight attendants have been in conversation for several minutes, huddled in the small galley of a Boeing 727. They have finished serving this jam-packed plane a late breakfast and, on this coast to coast flight, they now have some time to kick back and gab. The situation makes for involuntary eavesdropping. The one doing the most talking is a petite woman in her mid-thirties, I'd say, and her closely cropped red hair complements her electric green eyes. She is a dynamo of energy and confidence.

I am sitting in the aisle seat of the first row after the galley and could not avoid hearing this conversation if I tried. The talker has just described wrecking her car when she swerved to miss a cat crossing a rural highway. Running off the road, she missed the cat, but when she cut the steering wheel to get back on the pavement she lost control of the car and it tumbled down the bank on the other side, turning over and coming to rest bottom up. With her seat belt intact, she was still in place, but upside down. The seat belt saved her life, she said. "It is that simple."

It was hardly a time for vanity, but she noted that when someone stopped to help, her first thought was that "everything that had collected in the floor mats, which had never been vacuumed, was now in my hair." Since she currently has virtually no hair to speak of, one has to wonder if that is why she had it all cut off. It seems to me that a reasonable alternative would have been to adopt the practice of occasionally cleaning the interior of the car. Nevertheless, the hairstyle suits her quite well.

To my pleasant surprise the loquacious flight attendant moves to another topic and identifies herself as a sophomore in college, about to declare marketing as her major. She said that she really wants to major in art, but "I've got to earn a living. I only know of one person with a Fine Arts major who has done well, this guy who recently re-did our kitchen." In something of a non sequitur, she said that when she finished college she would quit flying and go to law school if she and her husband had enough money at that point to make it possible. Couldn't she go to law school as an art major?

I am intrigued most of all by the facile acceptance of the pragmatic career choice. What is it we want most of all? Her choice is not a bad one—she has a good marriage and keeping it so is a high priority. But do the two of them define their future primarily in dollars? Is the decision to study art a decision to live in poverty? Certainly the risk is there, and taking vocational risks does not come easy for most of us. How risky have my choices been? Not so great, really, but at least above the norm. But the young woman and I are in very different chapters in our life-stories. She has most of hers ahead of her and as far as jobs go, I am nearing the end of the book. But even if to a lesser degree, I still face the same questions. I could retire in a couple of years and fulfill my dream of writing full-time. But, God help me, I *still* think about the fact that doing so would reduce my retirement income. I really mean *God help me!* Help me and I will veer off the well-traveled road and, quite possibly, save my life in the process.

Northwest Airlines somewhere over the U.S., 1996

5. Taking the Next Step

The Delta flight to Birmingham is delayed, so we all sit and wait. Well, not all of us sit and wait. There is a tiny boy here who has in very recent days mastered the basic mechanics of walking. Perhaps I should say *running*. Once he gets to the point of standing upright on his feet, with or without adult assistance, he totters for a moment, leans forward, and begins to go. His legs do not yet understand exactly what they are supposed to do and this causes him to stagger as he starts. But when the momentum builds, as it did just now, he really moves. For balance, or maybe out of sheer exuberance, he holds both arms straight up, extends the fingers on both hands as wide as possible, and away he goes, his anxious young mother just a few steps behind him. So thrilled is he with his accomplishment that he will keep doing this until he is either restrained by his mom or falls exhausted.

Most of us cannot remember the experience of learning to walk. Riding a bicycle or roller skating maybe, but our first steps are too long ago. We know what it is like by watching it happen for others or by teaching our own children. Perhaps walking begins when we discover that we can pull ourselves up to a standing position by grasping the slats around our baby beds or getting our fingers into the webbing of a playpen. Then one day a parent holds us erect and gently moves her supporting hands back an inch or two. At first our legs collapse beneath us and we go fanny first to the floor. Before long, though, two people help us: one holds us up and the other stands a few feet away with arms outstretched to receive us. We see the loving face and hear the reassuring invitation, "Come on. Come to me." We lean in that direction, have the sensation that we are falling and extend a foot to prevent it. We do not fall! Instead, we move under our own power from one set of hands to another.

It is a wonderful image to remember and contemplate. We are dependent beings, able to move forward only on the basis of trust. It is something we should not forget. The environment around us at whatever age is filled with threatening possibilities. And if we live long enough, we will again reach the place where walking is precarious. Our loved ones will worry about the possibility that we will fall, knowing that they cannot always be present to catch us. Today I am in the prime of my adult life and, like my father and grandfather before me, I love to walk. It is one of my favorite things to do. But this child's delight has something to teach me which goes beyond the realm of the body to the life of the spirit. Sometimes the weight of my life seems too great and I think I might as well just go ahead and fall. The next time that happens I will remember this boy, and I will listen for Your voice softly saying, "Come to me" and, lifting my open hands above my head, I will lean toward You and take the next step.

Dallas-Fort Worth Airport, 1978

6. Something to Declare

Arriving by train and plunging into the teeming multitudes already populating the terminals at London's Gatwick Airport at 7:30 on a Sunday morning, it did not occur to me that I might, in a matter of minutes, be singing a familiar hymn with a small, international band of Christians. But that is what happened.

> *Praise, my soul, the King of heaven,*
> *To his feet thy tribute bring;*
> *Ransomed, healed, restored, forgiven,*
> *Evermore his praises sing.*

So we sang a few minutes ago, some one dozen souls gathered in the tiny chapel in the south terminal. I was just wandering about, saw the chapel door open and went in. A Salvation Army chaplain welcomed us to the "free church" service of prayer and praise on a September morning. Although I had peeked into a few airport chapels from time to time, I had never attended a service.

After we sang the hymn, we read together and aloud a brief affirmation from what I took to be a modern language collection of hymns and readings published by the Anglicans. We declared our common faith: that we were created by God and, through his son Jesus Christ, our sins are forgiven. We should therefore not be anxious or burdened by guilt. The chaplain then prayed for all who were at that moment somewhere in the air, bound for Gatwick Airport. He prayed for their safety and for ours. He asked God to set our hearts and minds at ease as we anticipate boarding planes and soaring away to our several destinations.

The theme of this brief service was timely indeed. A few days ago, a Swiss Air jet plunged into the ocean I am about to cross, abruptly taking two hundred and twenty-nine persons to their burial at sea. While there has not yet been any indication that this tragedy was the work of terrorists, they have certainly been active in recent weeks, bombing buildings and killing hundreds of persons in the hope of taking out as many of my countrymen as possible. That is why, I suppose, the security measures here today are the most stringent I have ever experienced. They looked at every item in the bag I have with me, even studying for some time three small bottles of pills. Then I was physically "patted down" to determine if I might have a concealed weapon or other contraband hidden beneath my clothes. Come to think of it, we are going to make quite an appealing target for terrorists: over two hundred people in an airplane decorated with the word "American" in large red, white and blue letters.

We are even now ascending into the sky over the Atlantic Ocean, passing 15,000 feet on our way to 35,000. This huge airplane wobbles and creaks as we move through the weather. But here is the gospel truth: my spirit is more settled now than at any point since I left Tennessee. Once again the hymns and songs of childhood come back and lift me up. And one of them reminds me in this moment that You are my Father and I therefore have more than one home to return to:

> *This is my father's world; I rest me in the thought*
> *Of rocks and trees, of skies and seas...*

London, Gatwick Airport, 1998

VII.

Tales of Ten Cities

It has been my great good fortune to spend my whole life working with young people. Five years after I graduated from college I went back to my alma mater as its chaplain. All the professors I knew and greatly admired were still there. It was a little hard to imagine that my new role as a spiritual leader on the campus might have reference to them! But it did. They accepted me as I was and, while I continued to learn from them, I soon had both pastoral and prophetic roles among them. I was twenty-six years old and still looked up to many of the faculty with something akin to awe. In those early years I still identified with the students to a fault, I suspect, but somehow I, and the students, survived.

My first year as a college chaplain, 1964, was the year that the first wave of the baby boom generation came to the campuses of America. Those campuses would never be the same again and neither would I. As I have already indicated, what we remember as "the sixties" was formative for me as a young campus minister who identified with that student generation and, to a significant degree, experienced the time with them. But I got over it. Many of my campus ministry colleagues did not get over it and continued to understand their calling in the light of those experiences. My father's generation was formed by the Great Depression and forever made reference to it. To hear them tell it, if you did not go through that experience, there was no way you could really understand what life is all about. For my generation of campus ministers, the sixties played a similar role.

But as student generations changed and the gap between my age and theirs widened, I was able to mature in my role and become more effective as a campus chaplain. Over the years more and more students have come to the campuses from difficult home environments. They look for adults they can trust more than they look for a chaplain who identifies with them as a pseudo-peer. So the passing of my own young adult years did not make me obsolete as a spiritual leader serving college students. I had to keep growing and changing. And moving from one campus to another in a different part of the country helped me to maintain my professional vitality. But, after a quarter of a century as a campus chaplain, my church asked me to take responsibility for leading the denomination's programs for all our campus ministers and students and I was ready for the change.

If it was difficult for my relatives to understand exactly what I was doing all those years as an ordained minister without a church, it was *impossible* for them to understand what I did during the last decade of my career. Then, I did not even have a chapel and most Sundays I woke up in a city far from home where I had gone to attend a meeting, consult with a campus ministry board of some sort, or speak at a conference of students or campus ministers. The early Methodist preachers were sometimes referred to as "traveling elders" because their work took them from place to place in a circuit of preaching stations. Well, I have certainly been a traveling elder in recent years. A general staff person for a large denomination has to be a frequent traveler. Although it is often a grueling process, it also has its rewards.

I enjoy meeting new persons on an almost daily basis, and to a growing extent I was still working with young people as intercollegiate student Christian movements came to life once more. But I also enjoyed being in different cities so often. I am not talking about visiting the tourist sites, but about the opportunity to experience the everyday swirl of ordinary citizens going about their daily routines. It still amazes me how quickly one can be in a rented car, negotiating a freeway in Los Angeles or standing in the midst of a throng waiting for a subway in New York. Or walking across a university campus in Illinois or lying down to sleep in a retreat center in St. Louis. This is the way my life was during the nineties and there was much about it that I enjoyed. I had many opportunities to look and listen to life, to practice the spiritual arts of an urban pilgrim. The following private prayers in public places reflect the inner life of a chaplain whose campus became the nation and, sometimes, the world.

1. Miami: Waiting for the "G" Bus

There is a couple of afternoon hours free in our chaplains' conference, and there is something I want to see before I leave Miami. So I have been sitting for several minutes at a bus stop on Northeast 2nd Avenue. And I have noticed that, when cars pass this point the drivers inevitably look at me sitting here on a bench beside the busy street. Just now a middle-aged woman was required to stop her car at the traffic light hanging above this intersection and when she immediately cast a cautious look toward me, I returned the glance as if to acknowledge my being noticed. Instinctively, she hit the button controlling the electric windows of her late model Oldsmobile. Although the window on my side was only down about three inches, she raised it two and repeated the procedure for the window next to her. Do I, a fifty-two year old university chaplain, look like an immediate threat to life and limb? Have all these years of ministry bequeathed to me a menacing demeanor?

Suddenly I remember—as strange as it seems in this tropical environment—that today is the twelfth day of Christmas and therefore the eve of Epiphany. Tomorrow is the day when we celebrate the arrival of the three strangers to pay tribute to the baby in the manger, whose birth they had discerned by studying the stars. It was an early sign that this child would have special significance for the whole world. Who were these strangers who had come, these astrologers from the gentile sphere? The tradition calls them kings, majestic figures from afar. But the basic notion is that the *child* is the one who is making an appearance; the celestial invitation has brought these wise men in for a purpose. It is to show them that in this child the Light of God is shining, and it is a Light whose intent is to illumine all of human existence if not the whole of creation as well. These strangers have been brought to the place as representatives of *the others*, that great company who live beyond the pale of Judaism. The Light shines for them—that is, for us—for all the strangers everywhere.

But here I sit beside the road, my mere presence unsettling to all that pass by. We are more strangers to each other, perhaps even to ourselves, than we have ever been. Will the darkness win and finally put out the Light? The cars go whizzing by, their drivers still cutting apprehensive glances in this direction as I and the school girl who has taken the other end of this bench crane our necks to see as far down the line of traffic as we can, hoping for the approach of a bus. She comes here routinely, she says, and she gives me assurance that the bus both of us want, marked with the letter "G," will arrive any minute now. And yes, it will travel in an eastward direction and if I stay aboard long enough it will get me to the ocean before the darkness falls.

A Bus Stop in Miami, Florida 1990

2. New York: The Beginner

I have just sat down on an airport bus in New York City, ready to go home. We are at Park Avenue and 41st Street, around the corner from Grand Central Station, about to set out for Newark Airport. Once again this marvelous city has spoken to my spirit in a surprising way.

Last night a group of us took the subway from Greenwich Village to 42nd Street to pick up discount theater tickets, have dinner, and see a play. As we got off the train and plunged into the mass of people moving toward the stairs, I heard music so familiar and so out of place that it stopped me in mid-stride. Looking around for the source, I saw a Hispanic man sitting in a chair in the midst of that rushing, dispassionate throng and playing an accordion.

There could be no doubt about it; the tune was a hymn I had learned, literally, at my mother's knee: "In the sweet by and by, we shall meet on that beautiful shore." For a very brief moment I stopped to listen and when the man paused I said to him, "I love that old song," and I dropped two quarters into the frayed cardboard box at his feet. He extended his hand to mine, and after a quick hand-clasp and exchange of smiles, I hustled to catch up with my friends who had been swept along in the crowd.

Now, the morning after, I had once again gotten off the train in that dismal tunnel beneath Times Square. Since the memory of the night before had not yet returned to consciousness, I was all the more surprised to be abruptly facing the same man playing the same song. *In the sweet by and by, we shall meet on that beautiful shore.*

Alone this time, and in no great hurry, I stood a few paces to the side and listened, wondering now if the man's entire repertoire were drawn from the old *Cokesbury Hymnal* I grew up with. Judging from five minutes of listening and a brief conversation, I reached the conclusion that his whole repertoire in fact consisted of only two songs! But the stunning thing was that the second song had also been a powerful influence in the development of my youthful faith. When he finished *Sweet By and By* he went directly into the other piece:

> *There are depths of love that I cannot know*
> *Till I cross the narrow sea;*
> *There are heights of joy that I may not reach*
> *Till I rest in peace with Thee.*

This hymn, which includes the words, "I have heard Thy voice," has been a distant echo in my heart all these years, shoring up my sometimes feeble sense that I have been *called*. This time, when he had finished playing the tune, I dropped a dollar in the box and told the unlikely troubadour that I have loved both those songs all of my life. In Spanish-flavored English, he told me that he was from Santo Domingo and that he was a beginner on the accordion. I do not doubt that he is, but he played the tunes well enough for me, and did so while simultaneously clicking castanets under one foot and shaking a tambourine on a hinge with the other.

"My mother told me that if I was going to learn to play the accordion I ought to play religious songs," he said. "She is in the church, and so is my sister and brother and my aunt. I go, but I am not a part of the church." I told him that my mother also taught me the same songs, but I did not tell him that I was in the church because it was time for both of us to get on with our separate agendas.

I did not determine whether or not the man knows the words that go with the tunes he plays, although I would assume so. Certainly, thousands of people who pass by him every day do not know them. A New York subway presents a fast-moving microcosm of all of the world's people, most of them in a hurry to get somewhere else. That is why anything remotely familiar stands out so much. We do not know each other and, let's say it, we do not care to. If anything, what we feel from each other is a vague sense of peril, and we do not remain in each other's presence any longer than necessary. "Stand back from the edge," a woman said to me last night in a surprising show of concern. "They are pushing people onto the tracks now. There have been five so far. Always stand a few steps back from the painted line at the edge."

Is it conceivable anymore even to imagine that one can still hear "Thy voice" or that we shall, all of us, gather one day "on that beautiful shore"? If not, why does the very thought flood my soul with feelings I cannot begin to describe? I want to laugh and to cry at the same time! I always feel inconspicuous in New York and I revel in the sense of being lost in the crowd. But Your agents are everywhere, and so cleverly disguised! Once more You have caught me with my guard down and, yet again, I surrender.

Airport bus, New York City, 1996

3. Indianapolis: The Eyes of the Heart

It has been my good fortune to spend the last two hours in the Indianapolis Museum of Art, and now I am sitting outdoors in an area called "The Garden for Everyone." As one enters this space he is greeted by an invitation: "You are encouraged to touch the plants, and enjoy their fragrances and textures." Once inside this circle of flowers and seated on a bench, as I am, you will notice that the words of Antoine De Saint-Exupery adorn a low wall: "It is only with the heart that one can see rightly; what is essential is invisible to the eye." At first I am struck by the thought that just outside a temple dedicated to the marvel of vision, someone has created a place of beauty to be enjoyed equally by those who are blessed with functioning eyes and those who are not. But I also wonder if, sitting in such a place as this, I might better understand my reaction to the works of art I have just encountered.

More often than not, my visits to art museums are unanticipated, added on to whatever agenda has brought me to a new city. These visits are therefore almost always constrained by time and I find myself looking for the highlights, the works of art that might be of particular interest to me. True to form, I went in the front door of the building behind me already wondering where I might find whatever Impressionist paintings might be there. After having a hurried look at those, I would move on quickly to find the contemporary works. During this rather focused itinerary I came upon a room devoted exclusively to Indiana artists and very nearly skipped it altogether. In my ignorance, I assumed that the Indiana room would contain a provincial collection at best and, further, that it would showcase works favored by whatever the major benefactors in the area wanted hung. What a stupid mistake my failure to enter that room would have been!

Standing in the Indiana Room, I jotted in the margins of the museum map the names of J. Ottis Adams, William Forsyth, and T. C. Steele for future reference. These are the artists whose works I will remember from this visit. All three of them studied in Munich before returning to their native Indiana to paint during the early part of this fading century. Now I am asking myself why an oil painting of several cows standing in a stream some fifty yards below a bridge, or one of a mother with two children eating a picnic lunch beneath a tree, should affect me as deeply as they did. The fact that these paintings are rather dark overall, in what I understand to be characteristic of the Munich style of the time, may explain the sense of power and mystery they convey. But here is the heart of the matter for me: these ordinary scenes from an earlier era suddenly seemed present and alive. I cannot find the words to express the feelings that still linger after this encounter. The scenes captured on canvas did not cease to depict events from the past, but some aspect of those long ago moments was still there; either that or these paintings were able to evoke the Mystery itself. I had an almost eerie sense that I had crossed a normally solid boundary: the strong dividing line between the past and present had been lifted for just one moment.

Within the last week or so, I tried to understand a single page in a recent book on the thought of John Wesley. I still do not fully grasp the point, but my father in the faith believed that God knows the future as well as He knows the past, and this foreknowledge on God's part in no way compromises the freedom of human beings. God knowing what decisions I will make in the future does not *cause* me to make those decisions any more than my knowing that the sun will rise tomorrow is what makes it come up. I do not really understand that sentiment and don't care one way or the other. But here is what struck me: the author concluded that what Wesley meant was that the past and the future are *simultaneously present* to God.

Occasionally, I try to advance my meager knowledge of the cosmos, but the sheer immensity of the physical universe defies comprehension. One cannot think for long about these things, about matter and space, about heat and light, gravity and motion and time and all the rest, without coming up against Einstein's ideas about relativity—which is not to suggest that I understand the concept! But I do understand that "What time is it?" is a question that has to be answered in relation to where one is. Time, in that sense is relative. So I wonder if, in the grand scheme of things, there is any difference between the past and the future. From God's perspective, maybe it is always *now* as John Wesley apparently believed. And maybe, just maybe, when one encounters a work of art that seems to transcend time and space, one is drawing very close to the Mystery that surrounds us in every moment.

When I look at a great painting (or see an old photograph) of an ordinary moment in time, I can be struck by an overwhelming sense that the moment in question still exists and this realization sometimes moves me very deeply. It is such an awesome experience that I believe I must be standing, however briefly, in what the theologian Paul Tillich called "the eternal now." I have just experienced such a moment in the Indiana Room of the Indianapolis Museum of Art. What these moments say about art is another whole topic and one that is no less interesting to me. But right *now* I rest a few moments in the Garden for Everyone and marvel at what my heart has seen today.

Indianapolis Museum of Art, 1997

4. Rio de Janeiro: God Help Me!

Here I am again, very far from home, absolutely alone, and unable to speak the language with which I am now surrounded. This time it is Brazil and a restaurant called Chaika, a very popular spot for lunch on this early winter Sunday in Rio de Janeiro. I think that I have ordered a cheeseburger (recommended by the tour books) but I am not certain that this is what I actually asked for as I pointed toward a line of Portuguese in the menu. It was also quite a challenge to tell the waiter that I did not want ice in my *agua*, a result accomplished only by the repeated movement of my arm and hand to simulate dumping the contents from the glass.

I now have the result of my order: it looks like a cheeseburger to the casual observer, but one who bites into it, as I just did, will recognize that there is chicken where the beef should be. Fortunately, the sandwich is quite tasty, so I have no complaint, and the fried potatoes are very familiar. This place is also said to have excellent cappuccino, so I will give it a try while I sit here a little longer and let the experiences of the last week say to me whatever they will.

One cannot visit Brazil without being struck by the stark contrast between the very rich and the very poor. Hundreds of thousands of our fellow human beings live in abject poverty in the *favelas:* neighborhoods of crudely constructed shelters made of whatever materials are available, from cardboard and odd pieces of sheet metal to wood and bricks salvaged from hither and yon. These dwellings are all jammed together into one ramshackle structure extending as far as the eye can see.

Now something strange and poignant has already begun to happen in this cafe as I write. I have heard singing from the television set that is suspended from the ceiling just above my head and to the left. I know the voice and I know the song. It is the late Roy Orbison singing one of his very popular songs, containing the refrain, "Anything you need, you've got it." On the screen, a score of apparently prosperous Brazilian teenagers are dancing to this tune and its lyrics. I suppose this is a Latin version of Dick Clark's *American Bandstand* program. Given the direction of my thoughts these last few minutes I feel that I am yet again knee-deep in irony.

Some of the favelas are near the wealthiest neighborhoods in this fabulous city. In the United States we do a more effective job of hiding the poor (or hiding from them) so that we may go about our business and our pleasures without being reminded of their presence and of the continually growing income disparity among Americans. And I might as well be ruthlessly honest here as my consciousness drifts toward a personal confession of guilt. Those of us whose rhetoric extols the virtue of helping the poor may be the worst offenders of all since our words demonstrate that we are well aware of the issues involved.

Here it comes. Minutes ago, as I was walking down the sidewalk looking for this place I was approached by a young woman with a child in her arms. Although I did not understand her words, her face told me with immense clarity that she was seeking help for herself and her child. Seconds before, I had passed a church where a mass had recently ended and another was shortly to begin. This anguished young mother had chosen a strategic location in which to beg for alms. It was a place where she would encounter many persons in some way related to Jesus Christ, that great rabbi who had said of children, "of such is the Kingdom of God." But when this woman brought her child forward to intercept my movement toward lunch, I did not stop. I kept right on walking even as I felt her tug at my sleeve as I passed.

I was afraid to stop. Yes, as absurd as it already seems, I was seeking to protect myself. Immediately before I left a conference in Piracicaba a few days ago, a Brazilian campus pastor had jokingly asked me, "What is your favorite hymn?" Others chuckled as I tried to understand the relevance of this suddenly interjected question. One of them finally explained the humor to me. "He has heard that you are going to Rio de Janeiro and he wants to know what we should sing at your funeral." This is indeed a violent city. And there I was as I came down the street, flouting the basic rules of personal safety by carrying a shoulder bag with valuable contents, marking myself as a solitary tourist and an appealing target for thieves. So I kept on walking. But there is no way under the sun to justify my behavior in the situation.

I must face the reality that, by any reasonable global standard, I am a rich man—a rich man whose words consistently favor the poor while his feet favor himself alone. Largely by accident of birth I live and move among the *haves* rather than the *have-nots*. Anything they need, Lord, we've got it. But that does not mean that I have no needs. I am a needy man in this moment. Right now I need more than forgiveness. I need more than the usual cheap grace we dispense to each other in the churches. What I most need now, as always, is a heart that is stronger than my instinct for survival. I need open hands more than I need a facile tongue to explain away my guilt. God help me!

Rio de Janeiro, Brazil, 1999

5. Houston: The Lesson for Today

Flying from Houston to see a friend who lives at the southern tip of Texas, strong images of the last three days begin to come back. I think first of the elderly man I talked to on a downtown street. Then I think of the rather overweight woman, missing her front teeth, who always seemed to be sitting on a low concrete barrier outside the entrance to my hotel. Both, I now suspect, have something to teach me and I want to see if I can discern what it is.

My conversation with the man occurred at a bus stop on Main Street after I asked him for information on how to get to the Galleria Mall by public transportation. The difference in our skin color is important to note as I review the exchange between us. After telling me which bus to take and where to get off, the man went on to describe himself as a "yard man" for a prominent citizen of Houston. He had spent the day working at the residence. Our conversation drifted to the scourge of violence in the city and he told me several hair-raising tales about it from his own experience. It then occurred to me that I should have heeded the strong recommendation of the hotel staff that I take a taxi to the mall. In fact they had told me that I could not get there by bus on a Saturday night.

To my surprise, but also to my satisfaction, this stranger saw me as his peer, perhaps because we were both trying to get someplace on city buses. Speaking of the lawless element among us he said, "You and me, we ain't got nuthin'. But they will rob us anyway!" Of course, his amiability was fueled somewhat by occasional nips from a bottle inside a thoroughly wrinkled paper sack. Soon, after again withdrawing the libation from the front pocket of his jeans, he extended the bag to me and said, "I am not prejudiced; would you like a drink?" I declined the offer to taste the unidentified beverage, assuming it to be some kind of fortified wine with a less than genteel name, like Red Dagger or MD 20-20. But, oddly enough, as soon as I had given my "no thanks" response, I had a twinge of regret, somehow suspecting that my decision had been unfortunate, that I had missed something significant in that street-side exchange.

As for the woman, how is it that a person of indeterminate age, but whose body loudly implied decades of deprivation, came to be spending her time simply sitting, most of the day and night, on a low concrete ledge outside my hotel? I had passed her several times before I realized that she was not there to sell newspapers or for any other apparent purpose. I acknowledged her presence as I returned to the hotel last night and received a broad smile in response. She was there again this morning as I left to go to an early church service and I jokingly asked if she had spent the night in that spot. She laughed and said that she had not done so. When I asked her if there was anything I could do for her, she said that, well, she would appreciate some breakfast. Since I actually had very little money in my pocket, I told her that I expected to find an automatic teller machine after the service and that I would soon return with some breakfast money for her, for which she gave me her thanks in advance.

So off I went to the nearby First United Methodist Church, the largest congregation in my denomination. To my astonishment the primary scripture reading for the day was the story of the resurrected Christ surprising his disciples early one morning. When he came to the lakeshore near the spot where they were fishing, they did not know who he was. At that moment he appeared to them as a stranger. It was only when he prepared breakfast for them and called them in from their boats to eat it that they recognized him. He did not heal anybody or preach a sermon or turn water into wine. He just ate breakfast with them and they recognized who he was. I could hardly sit through the rest of the service, so preoccupied was I with the stranger who, moments earlier, had asked *me* for breakfast. But when I raced back to the hotel corner, cash in hand, the woman was, for the first time, nowhere to be seen.

Just now, on this southbound plane, something extraordinary has happened. For several minutes I had paused in my writing to ponder the questions my journey has raised. Who was that man, that diminutive gardener who had vainly offered to share his wine with me on Main Street? And who was that unfortunate woman who asked me for breakfast and then vanished into the morning air? As if in answer to my questions, the pilot's voice broke into my reverie with an announcement about an intermediate stop which had somehow escaped my awareness. "Folks," he said, "we are beginning our initial approach into Corpus Christi."

Corpus Christi! A whole city that calls itself the Body of Christ! How powerfully I am reminded that You are with us still and that Your word comes to us in the form of flesh and blood. Our cities are bruised, broken, and often bloody. But they could be transformed by gratitude, by Eucharist. It is not impossible for Your people, all of Your people, to be in holy communion, to be made whole again. In this moment at least I am able to give You thanks and praise for Your Word to me through strangers. And as I close my eyes to hold back tears of profound joy, I imagine that I am again walking the streets of Houston. And I am saying to everyone I meet the same words. They are words I have said many times before and in many places: *Because there is one loaf, we, who are many, are one body, for we all partake of the one loaf. The bread which we break is a sharing in the body of Christ.*

Eastern Airlines over Texas, 1986

6. Albuquerque: A New Point on an Old Circle

Yesterday I walked and climbed for two hours among the rocks of the Petroglyph National Monument on the outskirts of Albuquerque. Over a hundred thousand years ago volcanic eruptions created a vast sheet of lava that broke into boulders of many shapes and sizes as it cooled. These fresh rocks tumbled about and came to rest, one upon another, down the slopes of many hills. Over time the surface of the rocks turned black through interaction with various natural processes: rain, wind, sunlight, and so on. Perhaps as long as three thousand years ago, the people living in this area began to use the dark surfaces as a kind of permanent blackboard—they drew pictures by scratching away the black veneer to reveal the lighter color beneath. In this way they etched into the rocks a great variety of figures: birds, snakes, cats, sheep, circles, human faces. Hundreds of these ancient drawings are still visible on the rocks today.

While the images on the rocks are associated with the Pueblo peoples' dependence upon, and reverence for, the forces of nature, it is not exactly clear what role the drawings played in the culture. They are not confined to a specific area to provide a focal point for worship; they are scattered randomly over hundreds of acres. A visitor to the Rinconada Mesa, which is not yet marked by signs to direct one here or there, must wander about and locate the images for himself. This adds greatly to the experience of wonder and discovery.

Scholars believe that the concentric circles that are found among the petroglyphs are a symbol representing *time*. We know that the people who made the drawings imagined time to be circular rather than, as in our conception, linear. While we think of time as having started at a point from which it moves forward in a straight line, for them the beginning could be represented by any point on the circle. A booklet distributed at the ranger station in the park says that the drawings could be thought of as prayers "which say that the time of the beginning is now." I think that means that one receives the gift of each new day as though it is the first morning of the creation. And in so doing one acknowledges one's utter dependence upon the world of nature and again resolves to live in harmony with it.

For the few days I have been in Albuquerque, I have risen before dawn to see the first rays of light begin to illumine the dark sky and announce the arrival of morning. The retreat center where my meeting took place is on a hill outside the city; the twinkling lights in the urban valley below us are a joy to see in the evenings and many still blink in the darkness before dawn. Facing east, a range of distant mountains becomes barely discernible as a radiance begins to appear behind them, slowly revealing their profile as the darkness wanes. But at the climactic moment, the sun seems to burst forth suddenly, sending light and warmth to a new swath of the Earth as it turns. Sunrise in the desert regions of the west is somehow different; it is an immediate and sensuous experience, received through the skin as well as through the eyes. As I imagine someone a thousand years ago, or even a hundred years ago, standing where I stood, greeting each splendid dawn, it is clear to me that time is indeed circular in important respects, measured out day after day by the rotation of this round Earth, and season after season by our orbit around the sun.

Time out for a reality check! My reverie has been interrupted by a reminder that right now the only light I am basking in is the fluorescent glare of the Dunkin' Donuts shop where I have come for morning coffee. And this far from home, it was quite a jolt just now to suddenly hear my name. In response, I looked up to see a smiling young woman with her hand extended to me. "Don, I'm Jessica. You are Don, aren't you?" I replied that indeed I was, but that I was surely not the Don she was looking for. Her glance back toward the front of the shop quickly revealed another guy with glasses and a gray moustache. Begging my pardon, Jessica went in his direction to keep, I assume, a business appointment of some kind.

This encounter took place to the great amusement of five male retirees having their morning coffee at the table next to mine. But their attention was quickly diverted to a scene just outside the large plate glass window: a petite and quite pretty young woman was about to enter a huge, bright red pick-up truck in the parking lot. The step up to the driver's seat was so high that the men chortled about her prospects of gaining entry to the vehicle, but I took the remarks to be a cover for their real interest in watching her make the effort. As soon as she was behind the wheel and backing out of her parking space, the men fell into a dispute about whether or not that particular model of truck is equipped with four-wheel drive.

I have recently announced my decision to retire in about six months. Will I soon spend mornings passing the time with my own circle of cronies? Nothing wrong with that as far as I can tell, but surely it is not for me. At the meeting I have just attended here in Albuquerque, my colleagues from around the country acknowledged my decision with many kind words. I was touched by their expressions of gratitude for my life and work, but also made freshly aware that their remarks were evoked by something that is coming to an end rather soon. And so, dear God, grant me this wish, that this ending is merely moving the dot to a different point on the circle. Let September 1, 1999, be the day my life begins again.

On that day, let me rise up while it is still dark and lift my eyes toward Your holy mountain, eagerly waiting to greet You and receive the light and the warmth.

Dunkin' Donuts, Albuquerque, 1999

7. Cleveland: Suffering the Children

It was my intention not to do today what I am now beginning to do. I do not have to write everywhere I go, and the plan was to have this day with no necessary agenda and no fretting about the problems confronting the world. So here I sit alone in a fine little restaurant, waiting for what I expect to be a lovely meal. But, God help me, I have begun to write. The day demands it.

A few days ago I realized that I had all but forgotten about an unused air ticket and when I called to check on it I learned that it had to be used within a week or be lost. Checking the destinations served by the airline in question, I looked for a city I was not familiar with which could be reached in an hour or so, and chose Cleveland. The art museum has a great reputation and I had never seen it. So I have spent most of this day in that vast and wonderful place. Indeed, there is so much to see that I initially decided not to pay the eight dollars required to view the special show titled, *Faces of Impressionism*. I love the Impressionist school, but initially I had thought, "Just portraits? I don't think so." But when I learned that the exhibit would remain open after the rest of the museum closed at five o'clock, I decided to take a brisk walk, come back renewed and give the show its due.

As I strolled through the galleries, really quite taken by all the faces in the paintings, I noticed a woman doing her best to enjoy the art while holding a somewhat squirmy two-year old daughter in her arms. The mother wore the headphones of an audio device that provided a narrative interpretation of what we were seeing, so she might not have heard every sound the child made. It did not matter, for as our paths crossed more than once it was clear that the little girl's interest was focused upon the doll she clutched to her breast, and to which she occasionally addressed happy little sounds I could not hear well enough to understand.

After a while I was distracted by a loud and angry voice from somewhere behind me. Turning around and going back several steps, I caught the last of a tirade from the lips of a furious, red-faced man I judged to be in his late sixties. "I'm sorry," the intimidated mother said. "Well, you should be sorry!" the man snarled as he whirled around and stormed away from her. When I asked her what had happened, she said the man had told her she had no business bringing a child into the museum and that the little girl's voice so disconcerted him that he could not concentrate on the works of art. To my reassuring words, the mother said that she was determined that her child would grow up to enjoy the finer things in human experience and, to that end, she would, from the very beginning of her life, feed her spirit as well as her body.

Now here is what got me. Really got me. Some of the most beautiful paintings in *Faces of Impressionism* feature children and sometimes children in the arms of their mothers! Mary Cassatt's marvelous *Susan Comforting the Baby* was right there on the wall before us! We had seen Renoir's hauntingly beautiful portrait of a girl, *Romaine Lacaux,* and so much more. And there in the midst of it all, we had our minds diverted by the arrogance of a self-styled connoisseur. He was so bent upon his personal evaluation of the paintings that he could not abide the presence of a real, flesh and blood child in the arms of her actual human mother.

Oh, Jesus! I may be angry, but You would not have been pleased by this spectacle either. You made a big point about our welcoming the children and now, two thousand years of church life later, we are still not showing them much in the way of hospitality. The fate of children today is a topic any sensitive person must push from consciousness to get through the days. All around the world children are neglected; they die of malnutrition and curable diseases; they get caught in wars and, in some cases, they are deliberately killed as a result of conscious military strategies. In the small African nation of Rwanda, 500,000 persons, including thousands of children, were killed in the space of 100 days. That is but one horrible example. I need not recall more except to confess that right now the word *Hiroshima* is pressing against my consciousness. Obviously, I do not place the angry man in the museum in the category of child killers. But the episode reminds me again that we do not place the children first as You so beautifully asked us to. This is our greatest sin and disgrace. What irony there is the King James edition of the Bible when it puts Your appeal for the youngest ones into the English of the time: "Suffer little children to come unto me, and forbid them not: for of such is the kingdom of God" (*The Gospel According to Luke, 18:16*).

I know I have to calm down, but maybe writing these harsh words will help me do that. The moral ambiguity of my respectable American life is almost more than I can bear when I think about it too much. And it is not exactly guilt that I feel; I know You don't expect that I will personally establish justice in the world. If You couldn't do it, I certainly can't. In some sense, it is already too late for that anyway; too many atrocious things have already happened and cannot be recalled and set right. But, if I am not to go mad, I must not be obsessed with these matters. Sometimes it is important just to eat, drink and be merry. But for me tonight, two out of three will have to suffice.

Sergios Restaurant, Cleveland, 2000

8. Prague: Watching the Clock

As a traveling denominational staff person, I can truthfully say that I have been prudent in the use of my employers' money. If anything, I have sought too little in the way of reimbursement when filing expense reports. This is not to suggest that I expect a reward for being honest. It is simply the case that I still have enough religion left to make me cautious in the stewardship of money I know to have come from offering plates. Nevertheless, one cannot always know in advance that a particular project or trip will, after the fact, stand up well under the scrutiny of cost/benefit analysis. And, sometimes, you just go where you are sent. While I am delighted to be in the magnificent city of Prague as I write these words, I know that my mission here has not exactly been a great leap forward for the church.

My work with young people in Russia will always be one of my fondest memories. It was on the basis of success there that I was sent here to the Czech Republic. But the situations are not at all comparable. In Russia I was helping to form a United Methodist youth organization from the ground up. Here, such an organization already exists and is dominated by such a conservative theology that I had little chance to make a difference. And, if that was not impediment enough, I made mistakes in speaking through my young interpreter, a high school student who was thrust into the role without advance notice. He performed remarkably well as far as I could tell, but I later learned that my choice of words presented major obstacles. For example, I talked about campus ministry, which is, after all, the business I am in. But the word *ministry* in this part of the world (and in most of the western world for that matter) refers to a government agency. So the young people not only could not understand what I was talking about, but also never quite figured out who I was or what I was doing in their meeting. Otherwise, I am sure I was quite effective!

As a frequent flyer it was possible for me to upgrade my cheap ticket and ride across the Atlantic in the luxury of the business class cabin. In addition to the wider seat and better food, I had an experience that could have prepared me for the realization that there are roles I am not suited for. Seated beside me was a vivacious lady with whom I soon fell into conversation. From time to time she made references to what she and her husband planned to do in Prague. Eventually, I asked her if her husband were on the plane and she said that he was. So I pondered whether or not it would be appropriate for me to suggest that I swap seats with him. Fortunately, he appeared in the aisle beside me before I got the words out. And the lady introduced me to her uniformed husband, the captain of the crew flying the airplane! Our seat assignments were fine just the way they were.

However harshly I judge my performance, the fact remains that I am here in Prague with my formal responsibilities completed. During two free days I have walked for miles, enjoying the visual spectacle of this beautiful city. And I have attended several musical events, choosing from among the many presented at various times of the day and evening. And, of course, I have visited museums and other sites of aesthetic and historical interest. But I surprised myself by returning for a second look at what may be the primary magnet for tourists visiting this place. Along with scores, perhaps hundreds, of people I watched a huge clock until it marked in its distinctive fashion the passing of another hour. Later I came back and watched the same event all over again. This clock, built into the base of the tower of the Old Town Hall, was constructed in the late 15th century, and has told a somber story ever since.

Just before the passing of each hour, the figure of a skeleton at the top of the clock rings a bell and turns an hourglass upside down. Both actions remind you that your time is running out. This is followed by a parade of rather grotesque figures representing Christ and the twelve apostles; each appears briefly at a small door and then moves on. Finally, at the top of the hour, a mechanical cock appears, flaps his wings, and loudly crows. This is a medieval spectacle, of course, and one can stand in the ancient town square and imagine the chilling effect upon the citizens, day after day and hour after hour. But, even today, you can tell that those of us who stand and watch with our cameras at the ready are also not entirely amused by what we see. We are, in fact, rather quiet as we stand and watch the drama of the clock.

Now I have sought refuge in a coffeehouse near the square, and have comforted myself with a warm cup of the brew along with a delicious pastry. Now I sit and wonder: should I be thinking of each passing hour as one step closer to my death and therefore nearer to being called to account for how I have lived my life? While that belief is still a central doctrine of the biblical faiths, it is enthusiastically affirmed only by those who are convinced that they have done whatever it takes to be spared on the Day of Judgment. But I cannot escape the suspicion that, in the Middle Ages at least, the idea was put forward basically as an instrument of power and control. "Do what we say or suffer the eternal damnation of your soul." Nevertheless, some notion of accountability for our actions still seems right to me. But, to tell the truth, it is not death that bothers me; it is *life* that stalks me with its incessant questions: Who am I? What is expected of me? Why is there so much suffering in the world? Why is there so much beauty on the earth and in the heavens above? Is God really with us and for us? The biggest mistake is either to evade such questions or to accept the easy answers that are available in such abundance. Insofar as there is an Answer, it is found only by living the questions—maybe by *loving* the questions—day after day, and year after year.

Cafe Slavia, Prague, The Czech Republic, 1996

9. Aberystwyth: Minding My Head

It is just after seven in the morning and this train is going clickety-clack in an eastward direction across the middle of Wales. The green pastures dotted with sheep are gradually emerging as the sun dispels a dense early morning fog. The scene gives me hope that my mind will also clear up a bit. I do not always understand why I do the things I choose to do, and now is a good time to ponder that question. When I told my host at a conference beginning in Birmingham this evening that I would arrive in the United Kingdom two days early and make a very brief visit to the coastal city of Aberystwyth, he (a native of Wales) replied, "Whatever *for?*" For the last few days I have been asking myself that very question.

The best explanation I have come up with goes something like this. One week ago I completed forty-two years in active service as a United Methodist minister. Most of those years were spent as a college or university chaplain and, although it was a deeply satisfying way to live, I recognized the chance to retire a little early and took it. The last decade of my work has been spent as a denominational staff person for campus ministry, a role that requires extensive travel. The conference I am bound for will bring down the final curtain not only on that portion of my career but also upon all that preceded it. That being so, it seemed a good idea to call "time out" for two or three days both to recover from jet lag and to just sort of vanish. Why not just get on a train and head for a place I have never been, never heard anything about, and the name of which I can barely spell or pronounce?

Even though this journey has not turned out particularly well, I am glad I took it. After waiting in the Atlanta airport for a couple of hours in the middle of the night and being told more than once that diligent efforts were being expended to repair something called an auto-throttle on the plane, I saw the pilot and crew leaving the area with their luggage. At about the same time we were told that sandwiches would be available for us shortly in a nearby meeting room. Aware that another flight was about to leave for London (mine was for Manchester) I raced down the corridor to see if I could get on it. I did. My luggage did not. Once in London, the airline assured me that when my bags arrived, they would get them to me in Aberystwyth, which they did, but not until last night. And, leaving from London rather than Manchester, it had taken me forever—via three trains and a bus—to get to the coast of Wales, arriving after dark instead of just after lunch, as initially planned.

The point is that all of this suited me just fine. I welcomed the circumstance of not being in control of the flow of events. The journey itself was my destination; I was glad I was not bound for a place where I would feel pressure to make the most of the time in order to see everything I should see. I savored the realization that I was not in charge, not expected to make things turn out well for anyone else. In spite of these low expectations, I found the place interesting. I walked all around the town, ate fish and chips at the waterfront, rode a narrow gauge rail line up into the forest, attended worship in the parish church and so on. There was more to see than I saw, but I feel no regret about it. I was where I was and I did what I did. And now I am going back to England.

At one of the stations where I changed trains on the way out here, there was an amusing sign above a low passageway. It said, "Mind Your Head." That word *mind* has several meanings. When I heard it as a child it was usually a verb meaning to *obey,* as in "Mind your mother." In that sense the sign might be an admonition to obey the dictates of rational thinking. But if I insist on reading it as a pun, which of course I do, the word has to mean *take care of* your head. I like the juxtaposition of thinking and caring. I suppose it is the theme of my whole life. Trying to think and to care with equal enthusiasm can wear you out, and I guess I would have to say that I took the early retirement option because both my mind and my heart were too tired to continue. But there is nothing like riding a train through the countryside to recharge one's mental and spiritual batteries. Thanks to you, O Aberystwyth, I am feeling better already.

Train from Aberystwyth, Wales, to Birmingham, England, 1999

10. Chicago: Trains of Thought

They told me it could be done, so I am giving it a try. Since it is not rush hour and there are therefore fewer trains, more transfers than usual will be required to go from Evanston to Midway Airport, but the total cost of the trip will still be $1.50 and I will see a lot of Chicago along the way. I am to exit this train at the Howard stop, then take the Red Line to Belmont. From there, I am to take the Brown Line to "the loop" in the heart of the city. Then I take the Orange Line out to Midway. The possibility exists that all of this will fail to get me to the airport in time to make Southwest's 1:00 p.m. flight to Nashville. But, as a friend of mine used to say, I am not late yet.

It is what most would call a dreary day today: overcast with gray and raining softly but steadily. There is no reason to think that the weather is going to change anytime soon. I guess I am in one of my moods since I chose to walk from Northwestern University, sans umbrella, to the main train station in downtown Evanston. My hair is not all that wet, but my feet are soaked; the most expensive pair of shoes I have ever owned, it is now clear, do not take to puddles very well. Worse, my trousers are wet from the knees down. But there is something about going against the grain of what prudence requires that sort of pumps me up.

When the train reached the Howard stop and folks poured out onto the platform, I approached a fellow passenger and inquired of her how to find the Red Line train. Her response was immediate and ferocious: "I don't know!" Her tone and facial expression said a bit more: "Get away from me NOW!" Fortunately, the next person I asked told me quite courteously that all I had to do was to walk directly across the platform, about twenty feet, and board the train that was already there with its doors open. I noticed that the angry young woman was a bit more familiar with the Red Line than I had reason to believe, since she had gone without hesitation to board it ahead of me. For whatever benefit it might be to her state of mind, I quickly walked on down the platform to enter a separate car. The train stayed put for quite a while, beginning to move just after I heard one rider ask another, "What is rapid about rapid transit?" It was a rhetorical question, asked with a smile.

We have just passed two cafes facing the track, one called the Heartland Cafe and the other the No Exit Cafe. If given the choice I would take the first one for sure. Although the name of the second place clearly owes its origin to Jean-Paul Sartre, it brings to mind a song by Hank Williams: "I'll Never Get Out of This World Alive." Oddly, the next thing that catches my eye is a cemetery whose perimeter comes right up to the tracks. Cemeteries in urban areas always give me a jolt; I suppose it is because in my experience they tend to project a rural ambience regardless or where they are located. This one has a really striking feature: the stone wall around it is topped with razor wire! Nobody resident there could get out, and there aren't many, as far as I know, who would be eager to get in.

The young man in the seat next to mine is listening to a tape recording via earphones. But the volume is turned up so high that I cannot avoid hearing bits of the lecture that has his rapt attention. It is religious in character and now and then I catch something about the necessity of submitting oneself to I cannot tell exactly what. The graphic designs on the pages of the book that is open in his lap confirm that the spiritual perspective involved is of Asian origin. It contrasts with the copy of *Christianity Today* that lies unattended in my own lap. Each of us in our own way is trying to find a way out of, or maybe into, this world.

The third stop has come and gone and here we go on the Orange Line toward Midway. We still have rather far to go to reach the airport and making my scheduled flight to Nashville is highly unlikely. This realization pleases me very much; I was beginning to fear that I would miss an excellent opportunity to wait.

Trains in Chicago, 1998

VIII.

Nashville Scenes

Nashville, for good reason, calls itself Music City. But thousands of people elsewhere think of it as the Methodist Mecca. The denomination's huge publishing house, and several other boards and agencies have long made their home in Nashville. The Southern Baptist Convention, the largest Protestant denomination in America, is likewise headquartered in Music City, as are several agencies of the much smaller African Methodist Episcopal Church. And Thomas Nelson, Inc., "the world's largest Christian content provider" publishes its bibles and popular devotional books in Nashville. More could be said, but this is enough to demonstrate the importance of religion among the institutions in the city.

Nashville's prominence as a center for higher education and the fine arts may be less well known than its roots in religion and country music, but the largest employer in Middle Tennessee is Vanderbilt University (when its hospitals are included). There are so many colleges and universities in the area that Nashville has sometimes called itself as "the Athens of the South." But the campuses do not tell the whole story. The Frist Center for the Visual Arts opened a few years ago, as did the wonderful Nashville Public Library in the heart of the city. *Musica*, a huge and stunningly beautiful bronze sculpture celebrating creativity in the arts, now stands at the entrance to Music Row. And a campaign is underway to raise 120 million dollars to build a state of the art home for the increasingly prominent Nashville Symphony. There is much more to the area's character and economy, but religion and higher education, including the fine and performing arts, are certainly among its distinguishing features.

All of the above having been said, it nevertheless remains true that Nashville is a city where music rules, and the music it is best known for is country music. It is important to understand that country music is actually a broad category that includes many distinct musical traditions such as bluegrass, western swing, folk, gospel, and so on. The most important element linking all this music together is its rootedness in the real life of ordinary people. Of course, country music is always in danger of losing its soul to commercialism, and that is certainly true today. But the authenticity is still there even if one has to look for it at times. At its heart, country music—as its name indicates—still embodies the rural culture of the South and the experiences of working people in the cities. Blend this music with religion and higher education and you have the basic elements that shape the special character of Nashville.

In my life the strain of country music that has been most important is usually called Southern Gospel. Its roots are in the churches of the rural South which provided much of the social life in the communities they served in earlier generations. People gathered to sing because it was fun as well as devotional in character. Although I was born and raised in a city, I inherited the rural spirituality that had shaped the generation of my parents. My mother played gospel songs on the piano all her life even though she had no formal training. From my childhood I sat beside her on the piano bench and sang those wonderful old songs with her. At times we would have a roomful of family joining in. Although I went on to develop a deep appreciation for the more formal hymns of the church, the influence of gospel music in my life has continued to the present day.

It has lately dawned on me that I love Nashville so much because it celebrates three of the primary themes of my own life: faith, learning, and music. I can say with assurance that my formation as a human being has been largely shaped by love of these things and the ongoing quest to reconcile the tensions among them. Of course it is human relationships, the love of family and friends, working with colleagues day after day, and concern for the welfare of strangers that give us meaning and identity. But all these relationships are informed by faith, knowledge and the songs we sing.

I moved to the Nashville area more than a decade ago to work for a United Methodist general agency concerned with higher education. Although I have been retired for a few years now our long anticipated return to Alabama has not yet occurred. Now that I have more time to enjoy all that Nashville has to offer, I am finding it difficult, if not impossible, to leave. I am listening to music, reading many books, working in my garden, taking classes for retirees offered at Vanderbilt, and still trying to plumb the mysteries of life and faith. Although most of my private prayers in public places were written while traveling, I find myself still writing them from time to time now that I roam a great deal less. The pieces that follow were all written in and around Nashville over the last several years.

1. Smiling at the Flowers

Today at lunchtime I was walking down West End Avenue near the Vanderbilt campus. As I approached the Holiday Inn, I saw ahead of me an old woman who was somewhat oddly attired. She wore an orange sweater with green pants, which was not all that unusual, but on her head she wore an old-fashioned green visor of the sort long ago associated with bookkeepers and clerks. More significantly, although she was standing at a bus stop, she had her back turned to the street and was looking at something in front of the hotel. As I drew closer I noticed two things: she was looking down at a bed of flowers, and she was smiling at them. Smiling at the flowers.

I was so taken by this woman, as florally dressed as she was, that after I had gone about thirty feet beyond her, I turned around to have another look. She was still smiling at the flowers. Hooked by the scene now, I circled back through the hotel parking lot to gain another view without being noticed. By this time the lady had made her own slow circle around the bed of flowers and she stopped about the time I did. Deliberately, she leaned way over and pulled a raft of red geraniums from the ground, roots and all! She shook the dirt away and placed the geraniums with, I now saw, the begonias she had previously plucked. Personally, I did not know whether I should write a poem or call the police. But I did neither. Instead, I just stood and watched as she made her unhurried exit, a metal walking cane in her right hand and a burst of red and pink cradled in her left arm. And she was still smiling at the flowers, *her* flowers now.

This woman may not realize it, but her aesthetics and her ethics are in a state of conflict. Nevertheless, for my part, I would not be too quick to make a choice between the two if I had to decide. I have known too many ethically charged up people who would have been better human beings if they had occasionally smiled at some flowers. And maybe stolen a few, pulling them up roots and all in broad daylight.

West End Avenue, Nashville, 1995

2. With Today In My Eyes

It is just a few days before Christmas and Nashville is as cold as Nashville gets. Something called the jet stream has brought us a premature taste of deep winter, a surprising pre-Christmas gift directly from the North Pole. But, undaunted, I have pried open the ice-locked doors of my car and made my way from Brentwood to a favorite place in the city. It is Provence Breads and Café, located in Hillsboro Village, a stone's throw from Vanderbilt University where I have an appointment in about an hour. The bread and the coffee here are always excellent and the probability of finding a delicious bowl of soup is always high. Once again, I have not been disappointed.

This is the sort of place that would have appealed to the Yuppies and no doubt now attracts whatever their contemporary equivalent is. Which is to say that the narratives here are almost as good as the food. For example, we are told that the coffee I have chosen, the Ethiopian Yergacheffe, is made from the same kind of Arabica beans chewed by monks centuries ago to keep themselves alert. As for the bread, the story is that the young bakers here are sent to the south of France to learn from their elderly counterparts in the villages. The soup, which I have now finished, contains not only tomatoes and fresh basil, but also a variety of mushroom the name of which I had never even heard until today. I do not need to mention that the honey, which I put in my coffee as well as on the bread, is from Switzerland.

But I have come here today for more reasons than the quality of the food and the ambience, and I have brought along my own chosen narrative. I am really here to think about Christmas and to be grateful for all the blessings of this year, and of this life. To that end I have brought with me a small book which contains Truman Capote's *A Christmas Memory*. I hardly need the text since hearing the entire piece recited has come to be one of the special features of the Christmas season. I heard a dramatic oral interpretation of the story this past week in the old Bellcourt Cinema just around the corner from where I am presently sitting. The experience is still strong in my consciousness and I want just to sit here for a while and savor it again.

There is one specific place in the recitation of *A Christmas Memory* that I want to return to every year; I want to see the words on the page and linger over them for a while. This is the situation: Buddy, who represents the author in his childhood, and one of his elderly cousins—with whom he lives—have gone into a pasture on the afternoon of Christmas Day. (Although we know it from other sources, the name of the cousin is never given in this story; she is always referred to simply as "my friend.") Year after year the two make kites to give each other as Christmas presents and go, as they have now, to the pasture to fly them. At this moment they have the homemade kites well established in the sky where they cavort like fish hooked at the end of the strings. Their dog, Queenie, has just completed her annual ritual of burying the large bone that had been placed on the Christmas tree for her. Buddy and his friend sit in the grass, watch the kites, peel and eat Satsumas, and savor their intergenerational friendship. It is a beautiful moment and, basking in their shared joy and contentment, Buddy's friend experiences a kind of revelation:

> *"You know what I've always thought?" she asks in a tone of discovery, and not smiling at me but at a point beyond. "I've always thought a body would have to be sick and dying before they saw the Lord. And I imagined that when He came it would be like looking at the Baptist window: pretty as colored glass with the sun pouring through, such a shine you don't know it's getting dark. And it's been a comfort: to think of that shine taking away all the spooky feeling. But I'll wager it never happens. I'll wager at the very end a body realizes the Lord has already shown Himself. That things as they are"—her hand circles in a gesture that gathers clouds and kites and grass and Queenie pawing earth over her bone—"just what they've always seen, was seeing Him. As for me, I could leave the world with today in my eyes."*

Oh, yes, yes, yes! Buddy's friend suddenly sees the essential Secret and it has been given to me as well to catch a glimpse of it today. Sitting here in the Provence Café I am suddenly in the presence of the Spirit. The curtain of time is parted just enough for me to catch a glimpse of God's eternal now and my soul is flooded with an indescribable joy. And already the vision begins to fade. It is always like this; such moments are rarely reached and never grasped. But when they come, one can only receive them gratefully and, most of all, trust them. As for myself, I can say right now with laughter in my heart, that I, too, could leave this world with today in my eyes. And it all would have been enough. More than enough for me.

Provence Breads and Café, Nashville, 2000

3. A Shower of Stoles

For about an hour I have been sitting alone in a small chapel in Nashville's West End United Methodist Church. I have never seen a chapel decorated the way this one is today. All around me—hanging on the walls and randomly draped over the backs of the pews—are brightly colored stoles that symbolize the professional order of ministers in The United Methodist Church. It appears that there are about three dozen of them and each has attached to it a typed narrative that tells how the original wearer has been affected by this denomination's discriminatory policies concerning persons who are homosexually oriented. Most of the persons represented by the stoles had to leave the ministry when their sexual orientation became known or when the pressure of leading a double life became intolerable. A few say, anonymously, that they are still pastors and still in the closet sexually.

Although The United Methodist Church's *Book of Discipline* declares such persons to be of sacred worth, it also asserts that the practice of homosexuality is contrary to Christian teaching. It says that none of its clergy may preside at a service in which two persons of the same gender enter a covenant to live in faithful union with each other. It says that no service of this kind may be held in a United Methodist church. And, needless to say, it declares that no person who acknowledges that he or she is homosexually oriented, and lives in a way that is consistent with that orientation, may be ordained to serve as a minister in the church. That is what this "shower of stoles" is meant to dramatize.

In addition to the stoles with their stories attached, boxes of Kleenex tissues have been strategically placed here and there on the pews. This exhibit makes people cry. I saw them wiping their eyes at a service in this chapel two days ago and, here alone on a Tuesday afternoon, I feel like crying myself. But I will not cry this time, and for a good reason. In just a few days, I will violate these unholy policies of the church in a public way, and the anticipation has already provided me a measure of emotional relief from the mean spirit that now rules the church I have loved my entire life. I look forward to presiding at a service of commitment in which two wonderful young women (both raised as Methodists) who deeply love each other will pledge to live together and support each other—in good times and bad—until they are parted by death. It will be a truly joyful and sacred ceremony attended by some two hundred people.

So today I am experiencing a curious rush of feelings, an unlikely mix of anger, sadness and deep peace. I am angry that willful ignorance and cowardice hold the balance of power among the leaders of our church—those who gather every four years to pass legislation. They do not, in my opinion, truly represent the spirit of the people in the pews. They think they do, but they don't. The people look to their leaders for information and guidance; most want to do in every situation what Jesus Christ would have them do. But their shepherds are afraid to feed them or lead them. I am sad because this state of affairs is nothing new. I began my ministry listening to Methodist leaders in Alabama trying to make the case for remaining a racially segregated church. Then as now, many of those who knew better did not say so. I have lived long enough to see the racial climate in the church change radically even if not all the problems have been solved. But here we are again, *officially* turning our back to a whole group of innocent people. As United Methodists, we have been tweaking our policies on homosexuality for decades now, trying to effect a compromise strong enough to hold the church together while keeping a carefully calibrated distance from the Holy Spirit.

So how can I sit here in the midst of these powerful symbols of exclusion, vent my anger in such harsh words and at the same time feel myself calming down inside? It is because I have decided—this time, at least—not to obey an ecclesiastical edict that makes a mockery of the gospel for which Jesus lived and died. Now, my dear Father in heaven, I hope You recognize that all of this writing is at heart a prayer directed to You. I thank You for these quiet moments in this chapel and for the lives that these silent stoles represent. I thank You for the Methodist movement that has shaped my whole life and given me my work. I will always be a Methodist in my heart of hearts. Our singing has made me who I am. But it is our determination to turn our faith into action that has given our church its unique identity. Please, please, please! Stop us before we completely forget who we are and where we have come from.

West End United Methodist Church, Nashville, 2001

4. A Flowering of Memory

I am arrested in my morning walk around Radnor Lake by six pink flowers on a wooden bench beside the trail. When I stopped to look, I saw that the cut flowers, on stems six inches long, had been laid adjacent to a small plaque which indicates that the bench is here as a memorial. Reading the inscription engraved on the small metal marker, I learned that the one whose memory the bench honors is that of a young man who died during his sixteenth year of life, and that his passing occurred fourteen years ago. Now I am startled by the realization that two small sticks—more like twigs and no more than four inches long—have been intentionally placed here beside the flowers, one on top of the other in the pattern of a Christian cross.

These images are all the more powerful because I know they were not placed here for me to discover. This is a private and deeply felt gesture, an act that keeps alive the bond between two persons unknown to me: one living and one dead. Nevertheless, it is not in me just to pass on by. So I have sat down on the bench, straddling it at mid-length, to contemplate what this humble offering of sticks and flowers might mean to a passing stranger. The sight of these things, so placed and arranged, brings tears to my eyes and I feel a kind of sweet sorrow for the loss of someone about whom I know only this, that his name is on one of the many benches in these woods. A part of what I feel arises from this overt confirmation of what I have sensed for a long time—that this forest is a holy place.

It is impossible to miss the resonance between this small altar and Robert Frost's poem, *The Tuft of Flowers*. The poet went out to turn the hay in a field that had been cut by someone else earlier in the day so that the hay might dry on the underside as it had on the top. As he began the task, Frost was musing on the fact that he had to work alone, just as the earlier man had worked alone. But then he saw that a tuft of flowers still stood in the field, having been spared the blade by the man who had cut the grass. It was an act the poet appreciated, and at that moment he felt that he no longer worked alone; the other worker was somehow present in the flowers he had allowed to stand. So also as I look at these flowers with the cross of twigs beside them my heart goes out to whomever it was who came to place them here in memory of a young man whose life ended much too near its beginning. There is a presence here and it has touched me today.

I would not have come this way at all had I not been diverted by a most intrusive form of technological innovation. After spending a few lovely moments in an eye-to-eye encounter with a deer beside the trail, I resumed walking only to hear a voice behind me cry, "Hey, good morning! How are you?" I turned back to learn immediately that I had not been addressed. A briskly walking man had just rung someone up on his cell phone and proceeded to chatter away as he passed me. At that point along the path, one has the option to take a short digression on a side trail that makes an arc up the hill and back down again. I chose it this morning to escape the manic sounds of the man with the phone. It was at the crest of the arc that I saw the bench and the flowers and sat down.

I am glad I was diverted to this spot even though my intention had been to keep my heart pumping all the way around the circuit of the lake in my customary manner. But my heart has found something else here, and the encounter is not yet finished. Just now I noticed three more flowers, identical to the others, lying on the ground behind the bench. At first I thought they belonged on top with the others and I bent to retrieve them. When I had the first one in hand, intending to return it to the rest, I saw that it was further along in the process of decay, as were the other two. So my unseen fellow pilgrim in these woods had also come here some days earlier and will no doubt return again one day soon.

The middle name of the young man who died is Adam, which is the Hebrew word for *man*. So in a sense he is not just one of us, but all of us. That being so, as I prepare to leave this place I will say a prayer not only for him and the one who remembers him so faithfully, but also for the rest of us, for the whole human family. Dear God, please don't forget us.

Radnor Lake, Nashville, 2001

5. Bread and Company

At last we have a rainy day in Tennessee, something that for months now has been rare indeed. But we woke up to the pitter patter this morning and right now it looks like it will remain, as some would say, "gloomy" all day long. But I say *good!* This is my kind of day and I have taken up a customary position near the large windows of a bakery/cafe and now have before me a rich cup of coffee. So let the introspection begin!

Yesterday at church we celebrated All Saints Day even though the actual day, November 1, was last Wednesday. It is a day for remembering. Our pastor read the names of all the members of our large congregation who had died during the year. As each name was called a long-stemmed white rose was placed in a tall, clear vase on the altar table. Then we all had the opportunity to stand and say the name of any person now dead who had been dear to us. When all that cared to had called out a name, a rose was added to the bouquet for all of them collectively. It was a deep and emotionally gratifying ritual, followed by the Eucharist in its full significance as "the communion of the saints."

So here I am on the first Monday morning in November and still in a mood to remember. (It occurs to me now that I have chosen an appropriate place to reflect upon All Saints Day: a bakery called *Bread and Company*.) The person who has kept moving to the center of my consciousness the last few days is someone I never met. A philosopher, he wrote many books—only one of which I have ever had in my hands. That one I ordered after seeing a small ad for it in a highbrow magazine. It is not a philosophical book, at least not directly. Its title is *Born to Sing: An Interpretation and World Survey of Bird Song.* I ordered it because, when I was a student at Emory University forty years ago someone pointed to a professor riding by on a bicycle and said, "There goes Charles Hartshorne, the famous philosopher. Did you hear that he is leaving Emory for the University of Texas? The rumor is that he accepted the position because Austin is a better place for watching birds." We chuckled and that was that. But the comment came back to me decades later when I saw the ad for the book and I ordered it.

More importantly, about ten years ago I became acquainted with someone who attends the First Unitarian Church in Austin and who happened to mention that Professor Hartshorne was a member of the congregation. I was surprised to learn he was still alive and active in the affairs of the church and the Austin community, and I told my new friend the Emory anecdote about him and how I had found and purchased the book about bird song. When the philosopher died in October at the age of 103, our friend cut out the article about him from the local newspaper and sent it to me. I have the article with me this morning, along with *Born to Sing*. This must have something to do with my private observance of All Saints Day, but I am not sure what. What I am sure about is that these rainy day reflections will finally turn into some kind of prayer.

The obituary article says that Charles Hartshorne was the principal founder of what is called "process theology." This is a school of thought that assumes the existence of God, but does not accept the classical idea that God is all-powerful, all-knowing, and unchanging. God's perfection includes change; God *responds* to what is going on in the universe and to what human beings do. The most remarkable statement in this announcement of Professor Hartshorne's death quotes him as saying, "each person's thoughts, feelings and experiences are eternally and vividly remembered by God." Can this possibly be true?

Dear God, do You really know us so well? Each one of us? And are You in fact going through a process of becoming, just as we are? Initially, at least, I like the sound of this. If You are still growing and changing, maybe there is hope for me. I am in the early stages of becoming an old man and my biggest temptation now is the sin of inertia, just ceasing to make the effort which change requires. Don't let me lapse by slow degrees into a traditional pattern of bored belief and conventional behavior. I want to be more like You; I want to keep on changing and growing. In my heart of hearts, I know I want to fly. I want to sing. I want to give You something to remember me by.

Bread and Company, Brentwood, Tennessee, 2000

6. Thursday Love

I do my best to escape the blaring, glaring presence of television. But in this society that is an elusive goal indeed. Right now I am in a large room in which dozens of people wait to be called for various medical tests to be performed in the laboratories of a local hospital. In my case, I am here for a chest X-ray as part of an annual physical examination. Placed at front and center like an altar, the television is giving us the Oprah Winfry show whether we like it or not, and it is clear that most of us have other things on our minds. Sitting as far away from the tube as I could get, I finally failed in my studious attempt to ignore it. I failed because I kept hearing the word *love* spoken by a guest on the show. It was when I heard her declare, "I am love" that I finally gave up and began to look and listen.

There is a new word to describe what I am hearing: psychobabble. Anybody who cares to do it, and is sufficiently entrepreneurial in motivation, can attract some attention as an expert on what folks need to do to find fulfillment. As I understand it, Oprah's manic guest is claiming that love is within us and not outside us. Our first task is to get our love focused upon ourselves. "If you don't love yourself, why would anyone else love you? Just love yourself and love will bring more of itself to you. When someone enters a relationship with me, it gives me a new experience of myself." The practical application of this theory makes some sense. The guest is telling the women who listen to the show that they don't need a man to tell them they are lovable. Many women enter a relationship with a man, she says, thinking they can change him and end up feeling like a doormat. "If it has webbed feet and quacks, it is a duck. But women will say he ain't no duck!" The moral of this argument is that "it is wrong to reach out" to another person in search of affirmation.

Oh dear God! What a perversion of Your gospel we are hearing this afternoon. You see me and know me as I am, and it is clear to both of us that I am not an entirely lovable person. But You love me anyway. In my childhood I was taught to sing, "Oh, how I love Jesus, because he first loved me." That's not a complete theological statement, but it provides a strong foundation: love comes to us not from within, but from without. Genuine love, love that can survive the test of time is responsive love, love that is evoked by the experience of being loved. My parents always loved me, my wife has loved me for half a century, my children love me, and maybe there are a few more that also love me. That has made all the difference. I know that not everyone has been so fortunate. But the sense of being loved is what has given me my mission in life. Those of us who have received a lot of love are called to give that love to others. And I am not talking mush here.

Practically speaking, working out the implications of love for others is the most difficult job there is. It is difficult because, not unlike Oprah's guest today, we would rather love ourselves. But "self love" is an oxymoron; love, by definition, requires the presence of another.

Suddenly I remember that this is not just Thursday, it is Maundy Thursday. And for the first time in memory I do not have to go to a dictionary to remember what "Maundy" means. It is from a Latin word that means "commandment," the same root that gives us "mandatory." Maundy Thursday is in the Christian calendar to remind us that we are *commanded* to love each other. When asked which of the commandments is greatest of all, Jesus said that we could keep all the commandments just by loving You and loving each other. And Your beloved son demonstrated what he meant by kneeling down and washing his disciples' feet. Psychobabble does not understand this kind of love. Maybe I don't understand it myself. But I think you command us to love because it is something we must do if we are to find meaning and joy in this world. When they X-ray my lungs in a few minutes I should ask them to have a look in my heart as well to see how much self-giving love is there. I won't really know how healthy I am until that assessment is made.

Centennial Hospital, Nashville, 1995

IX.

Alabama Bound

It has been said that the first forty years of life are text, and the rest is interpretation. I believe I was putting down text a little longer than that, but I know for sure that the older we get the more we turn our attention to the interpretation of our past experiences. We ask: How did I come to be who I am? What were the formative experiences of my childhood and youth? What factors led me to make the vocational decisions I made? I am not sure we ever have complete answers to such questions. But I do know this much, that in elementary school I learned to sing a song about my home city of Birmingham, Alabama that contained the words, "She has made me what I am." Looking back after all these years I can still sing that song and, indeed, still make that affirmation. She has made me what I am.

Like many others who were born and raised in the South, I can be rather defensive about it. Early in my tenure as chaplain of Birmingham-Southern College, I attended a national gathering of college chaplains. While there, a chaplain from a campus in the northeastern part of the country said to me, "I would like to work on a campus in the South sometime, but I know I would not last three months." What he meant was that he would be so sensitive to issues of racial injustice, and so courageous in his stand against it, that folks would just run him off. The clear implication was that since I was still in my position, I did not possess those sterling moral attributes. Well, I had my problems with both the church and the society I grew up in, and I still do. But I would not go back and change the time or place of my birth or the cultural ethos I was raised in if I had the opportunity.

By today's standards, my life has been remarkably stable. When I was just a few months old, our family moved to a house two doors up from the one I was born in, and I lived there until I got married at the age of twenty-one years. With other children from the neighborhood I walked to Minnie Holman School. I still

118

remember the names of every teacher I had there, and when I saw a picture of our eighth grade class a few years ago, I could call the names of every boy and girl in the photo. In that group stood the girl I was already in love with and to whom I have now been married for forty-five years. Most of my childhood chums went on to Woodlawn High School, and after that a few of us went across town to earn our degrees at Birmingham-Southern College. While I was a theological student at Emory University in Atlanta, I commuted to north Alabama as a student pastor, and when I graduated, my wife and I returned to Birmingham where we remained for ten years.

Although the pattern of my life looks very conventional indeed, underneath it all there has been great intellectual and spiritual turmoil. Racial injustice was indeed at the heart of it all, but I find that I no longer wish to take the easy road of characterizing Birmingham and Alabama as a whole in terms of the worst aspects of their history. Growing up where I did, one saw not only the human consequences of racial bigotry and the associated exploitation of ignorance and fear by unscrupulous politicians; one also witnessed the unsung heroism of those who, in various ways, worked in behalf of a better future. The same dynamics were at work in the religious sphere. The culture was saturated with piety and that is what turned my heart at an early age in the direction of ordained ministry. But as soon as I started down that path I found it littered by boulders of doubt and disillusionment: the church was a very human institution indeed. But here again, I am grateful for the frustrations I had to cope with and for the presence of so many folks who walked before me and with me on the same journey.

I think I am a walking testament to the value of education. The high school class that made the most lasting impact on my life was the study of Latin. Even though I was a mediocre student at the time, studying Latin began my lifelong fascination with words and language. But I know beyond doubt that my life has been decisively shaped by my undergraduate education at Birmingham-Southern College. I have met many college graduates who never darkened the door of classes that formed the required core of my academic experience in a liberal arts college related to The Methodist Church (before a merger added the word "United"). I recognize that there are different approaches to education and that some programs must of necessity focus upon scientific and technical subjects. But liberal education gave me my life as well as my living, and that has made all the difference for me.

Participation in a male chorus called the Warblers Club was one of the highlights of my years at Woodlawn High School. We began our annual minstrel show with an "Opening Chorus," a medley of song and dance. One of the pieces in that group of songs went like this:

> *I'm Alabamy bound*
> *There'll be no heebie jeebies hangin' round*
> *Just gave the meanest ticket man on earth, all I'm worth*
> *To put my tootsies in an upper birth*
> *So when that choo choo sounds*
> *You'll know that soon we're gonna cover ground*
> *And then I'll holler so the world will know, here I go*
> *I'm Alabamy bound!*

It is my belief that one could not find an alumnus of the Warblers Club, no matter how advanced in years today, who could not still sing this song. I know for sure that while I may not be bound *for* Alabama, I'm certainly bound *to* Alabama. She has made me what I am. It is fitting for me to bring this book to a close with a few private prayers related to the place of my origin.

1. At the Edge of Dividing Creek

It is noon on the first Sunday of November, traditionally observed in the churches as All Saints Day. How odd, then, that I am sitting on the bank of Dividing Creek rather than in a church pew someplace. It took a couple of hours of meandering along first one rural road then another before I found this stream of water that separates Somerset and Worcester counties on the Eastern Shore of Maryland. I am here because I wanted to locate the general area where Richard Shockley lived after he arrived in colonial America from England in 1671. I have seen documents, including a plot map of various properties—including his—that say he lived near a branch of Dividing Creek somewhere not too distant from where I sit.

Until this year, no one in my line of the Shockley family knew where we came from and, as far as I could ever tell, it was not of great interest to them. So it came as a total surprise to me that, after asking a few questions on Internet genealogy sites, a correspondent sent information that enabled me to trace my ancestors back to Maryland and to Richard more than three hundred years ago. When I learned that there is a major genealogical research center at the University of Maryland, Eastern Shore, in Salisbury, I decided to celebrate the freedom of retirement by travelling to this area for a few days. It has been fun, and sitting beside Dividing Creek this morning is a nice way to conclude the experience.

Although I initially shared my family's lack of interest in genealogy, I at least wondered how the generation ahead of mine came to be living in rural Alabama. Now I know that one of our ancestors fought in the American Revolution and that, along with other veterans of the war, he was rewarded with a grant of land in Georgia. He and his family came down to claim their prize and, eventually, some of the clan moved on to Alabama as land there became available for settlement. So I now know something about my roots and they reach far deeper into the American experience than I ever imagined. And, after a lifetime of being told I have an unusual name, it is nice to discover that, in this part of Maryland at least, there are *hundreds* of people who share my surname.

But why take the trouble to find this remote spot today? The most obvious reason is that searching for this place has been an enjoyable little adventure. But the fact that I have found Dividing Creek on All Saints Sunday suggests that there may be something more. Lately, I have been looking back over my life and trying to understand the influences that have shaped my identity as a person. In this process I have gained a powerful sense of the fact that each of us stands in a long line of generations. It is a line that never stops moving and its destination is always the same. My father has been dead for more than a decade, and my mother finally had to leave their beloved country home. Last year we celebrated the birth of our first grandchild. I am moving to the front line of the generation parade and the experience is real and deep.

These woods are beautiful today. Some fall colors linger on the lower trees and shrubs, while the taller trees have dropped their leaves already, providing the soft brown carpet I am sitting on. But I cannot understand why Dividing Creek, rather shallow at this point and flowing gently, appears to be so dark. I believe it joins the Pocomoke River downstream and I recall reading that *pocomoke* is derived from Indian words which mean black or dark river. It is a natural phenomenon that I cannot understand or explain. Perhaps the streambed is lined with leaves that the process of decay has darkened. I am sitting at the base of a tall, solitary pine tree and just now a passing breeze causes the green boughs above my head to whisper. It is a sound I have loved all of my life and, as always, it gives me a reassuring sense of being at home.

On Maryland's Eastern Shore, 1999

2. A Small Cloud of Witnesses

Aunt Edrie Mae died last Tuesday. With heavy hearts, we drove from Nashville to the tiny town of Five Points, Alabama, to attend the funeral. As soon as we arrived at the house, which was full of family and neighbors, I realized that I had failed to anticipate something that should have been obvious to me. Almost everyone I greeted, whether kin or friend of my aunt, asked me if I would speak at the service which would begin in two hours. And already we were being urged to fill our lunch plates from the large table laden with food brought by the community in the customary way of closing ranks when its circle is broken by death. I would have to eat, and I would have to speak. There would be no opportunity to prepare.

Within minutes of our arrival I had another surprise. The elderly friends and neighbors who had gathered, few of whom I could name, seemed well acquainted with my life and career. One, a man who had lived just across the road for many years, spoke with tears in his eyes about how much my "example" had meant to "all of us." This told me of course that Aunt Edrie Mae had spoken of me through the years to her neighbors and, no doubt, at church gatherings. She had called their attention to things I had written in the print resources distributed by our church. Here was a circle of people, virtually unknown to me, who had long taken an interest in my life and, I am quite sure, had included me in their prayers from time to time.

For my remarks at the church, I drew upon a rich trove of childhood experiences. More than once my cousin Aubrey and I had come when we were small boys to spend a summer week with Uncle Julius and Aunt Edrie Mae who had no children of their own. During those times we had the run of their large country store which, in addition to its role as a provider of goods, was the center of community activity on weekdays. People of all ages were continuously coming and going and sometimes simply sitting in chairs around the dormant pot-bellied stove or playing dominoes at a table out front. We loved to be there, not just because we could help ourselves to candy, ice cream and soft drinks (sometimes pouring a bag of salted peanuts into a bottle of Royal Crown Cola) but also because there was something strange and mysterious about the place. This was particularly true in the back of the store where huge sacks of feed formed little mountains that could be climbed by small boys. The experience was enhanced by the thick, sweet aroma rising from the mound of sacks.

At the service it turned out that the persons who one after another had asked me to speak had given me the words to say. I spoke about a new realization, growing even as I stood in the pulpit and looked into the gathered faces, that I had been surrounded in my childhood—and in later days as well—by many aunts and uncles who had an interest in my life. This network of love and support was not so apparent to me in my youth or even in young adulthood. It is only by being forced to look back that I have now become consciously aware of its existence. And, in behalf of my siblings, all our cousins, and myself I expressed gratitude for all the love that surrounded us as children. Now, a few days later, I have a strong sense that I have not overtly reciprocated this caring as I should have. I think I know why.

The culture that initially formed me frowned upon pride to an unreasonable degree. Even though it is far more complex than it sounds, humility, or at least the appearance of it, was among the greatest of virtues in the piety-saturated ethos of my childhood. This observation can be summed up by the ubiquitous recipe for joy: **J**esus first; **O**thers second; **Y**ourself last. I recognize the irony in the realization that my attempts to honor that formula made me reticent to such a degree that I have not always been able to receive and be nurtured by "the communion of the saints." That is to say that I have characteristically underestimated my significance to other people. That is why I was surprised to learn that Aunt Edrie Mae's friends were not only familiar with the path of my life, but also *cared* about me and felt they had a stake in my development.

So I have learned something today as I revisit our trip to Alabama. I have a new sense of connection to the generation just ahead of my own. And now I give thanks for all they have meant to me; indeed, for doing so much to enable me to be who I am. And, in the time remaining, dear God, help me to be a little bolder in my love and support for them.

At home in Brentwood, Tennessee, 1993

3. The Boy Boxer Gets Up Again

The passage in Pat Conroy's novel, *The Great Santini,* was so powerful I had to close the book and ask myself why it affected me so. The scene was the parking lot outside a high school gymnasium. It was early evening and the names of the boys who had made the basketball team had just been announced inside. Fathers were in the cars parked outside, waiting for their sons and for the news. The young hero of the novel, having just got good news himself, paused at the top of the stairs leading down to the parking lot to savor the moment. And, precisely then, he heard from one of the cars below the sobbing of a boy in his father's arms.

It has been years now since I read the novel and was brought up short by the scene I have just described from memory. But the recollection still brings with it a powerful emotional punch and, as always, it still evokes a raw memory from my own childhood. My flashback is not about failing to make the cut of a basketball team. And, in my recollection, I am not a teenager, but a small boy. It is a day or so after Christmas and two families are seated in a variety of chairs around the perimeter of a small, over-heated living room. The home is half of a single story, cinder-block duplex in a housing project in Birmingham in the 1940's. My younger cousin and I have been coaxed into the middle of the circle where toy boxing gloves (a Christmas gift) are being laced to our small hands. Although my cousin is taking this in stride, I am utterly bewildered by the situation. You—my parents, my uncle and aunt—you want us to *hit* each other? You are going to enjoy this?

After the reluctant exchange of a few blows, I began to cry and thereby bought my way out of the situation at the very high price of humiliation and apparent cowardice. But, while it was not a rational decision at the time, it is as clear to me now as it was then that what I felt in those moments had little to do with hurting another child or getting physically hurt myself. The *situation* had already wounded me and, although I did not know it at the time (no one knew it at the time), it was a real wound of the sort that never completely heals. Some wounds go deep precisely because they are not intentionally, or even consciously, inflicted. There I was, at the center of that expectant circle of faces, surrounded by those whose emotional support meant life or death to my spirit, and everything I had learned from them so far was suddenly withdrawn. Now they wanted me to hit my cousin and they wanted him to hit me. And for no reason other than the prospect of entertainment.

Off and on for many years now, and when I least expect it, something makes this old emotional wound bleed again. Not often, mind you; I am not obsessed with it by any means. Something triggers it. Something like the Conroy book touches that sensitive nerve which links fathers and sons and suddenly I am a child again and once more in that circle of perplexity and pain. Ironically, this memory is brought back today by a beautiful family scene that I chanced upon just moments ago.

It is New Year's Day and, following a custom of many years standing, we are at Lake Guntersville State Park with three other couples, nurturing the bonds of friendship which have linked us together for decades. But this holiday has been different. For the first time, it was so cold that we were denied access to the golf course when we arrived two days ago. And then it snowed, blanketing the whole area under a coat of pristine white. As cabin fever began to set in, I decided to go for a solitary walk in the snowy woods, following a trail that led me at last to the golf course, then here to the lodge where I sit, think, and write.

As I started out along the fairway leading to the ninth hole, I heard cheerful voices ringing out ahead of me and soon saw, still in the distance, a young couple with a small daughter, maybe three years old. I moved on a little closer and took up a covert position in a pine thicket to observe the scene. Mom and Dad were taking turns sliding down the slope that led up to the green, sitting on a piece of cardboard for a sled. I was close enough to figure out that, although she squealed with delight as her parents took turns zooming down the hill, the little girl was apprehensively declining their repeated invitations to join them on the ride. After a while, Mom went to retrieve something from the car parked nearby as Dad slid down the hill again. The little girl carefully walked down the slope as her Dad started back up with the cardboard. Meeting her half the way up the hill, he had the idea that the child might risk a shorter ride and he was right. She sat securely between his legs and down they went. As soon as they reached the bottom, she simultaneously jumped up and began to call with all the voice she could summon, "Mama! Mama! Did you see me?" The response came right back, "Yes, I saw you. Yes! What a big girl you are!"

Alone and out of sight among the pines, a little tremor passed over me and shook loose a single tear that made a warm streak on my cheek as it ran down my face and off into the snow. It was then that I thought of my father. He was born on New Year's Day of 1904, so today is his birthday. A sweet, quiet, and gentle man, my father loved me very much and I loved him. He was no tyrant like the great Santini. And, of course, he never knew about the wound I have described. I don't think I knew about it myself until, well into adulthood, it popped to the surface when I first read the Conroy novel. You can wound the spirit of another person without intending to and without ever knowing that you did it. In my mature years now, I know all too well that I have been on the sending end of this exchange as well as the receiving end. That is just the way life is.

Although I have spent my life in the church, I no longer have many certainties. But I do know this much and it is something I live by: we are saved by grace alone. At the heart of things there is an Immense Compassion which rises up to meet us when, in whatever way, we lose our traction on the ground beneath us and begin an uncontrolled descent to we know not where. In the midst of such helplessness, something always stops me, saves me. From way down deep inside a soft voice rises with reassurance and affirmation. "I see you," it says; "yes, I see you and I love you." And in those precious moments, father, I know it is your voice I hear.

Lake Guntersville State Park, Alabama, 2001

4. So Much Like Me

How can one feel removed from that with which he is most familiar? How can one be haunted by the awareness of a hollow place at the heart of an important relationship? How can coming home make one feel like a stranger?

This is my alma mater and I have returned for the umpteenth time for the annual conference of the Methodists in North Alabama. I was born and raised in Birmingham; all of my children were born here. I lived on this very hill as an undergraduate student; I served as chaplain to this college for eight years of my life. I have been a Methodist since I was baptized in childhood. My feet are standing on the very roots of my existence. Why then am I sitting alone tonight in this austere dormitory room and feeling like crying?

In recent days I have reaffirmed my vocation as a United Methodist minister by backing out of a door already open to me in academic administration. After twenty-five years, my call to be a minister is intact. Then why am I uneasy around ministers? Do I make other ministers uncomfortable? Most others in this profession seem somehow more certain, more secure than I am. Do they think I am more certain, more secure? Maybe this is the heart of the matter: it is certainty itself that makes me uncomfortable. There is so much certainty here this week that I have to seek shelter in solitude.

I can't get away from the notion that faith that does not embrace uncertainty within itself is not faith at all. When one loses uncertainty one loses faith; what remains may be belief, but it is not faith. Maybe that is my problem: way down deep I do not find it possible to believe. Nevertheless, I know that at the core of my being I am pulled in a homeward direction, even as I am unable to conceive just what and where home might be. To trust that tugging at my heart and follow it is what faith means to me.

Was George Herbert right in that little poem, *The Pulley*, that You have deliberately withheld from us one particular gift, the gift of *rest*? Is my uneasiness in these surroundings a sign of Your wish to draw me closer to Yourself? Is it Your design to deny me comfort in all the catechisms and creeds? However it happened, my inability to be a believer in a conventional way has only quickened my love for this life and this world. And it has made my faith strong and deep. But I still feel alone in the midst of so many people so much like me.

Margaret Daniel Residence Hall, Birmingham-Southern College, 1979

5. What You See Is What You See

On the rare occasions when I return to my alma mater, Birmingham-Southern College, I like to spend a few minutes here in the library. I come not to look at books, but to see a certain group of paintings that adorn the walls. I am speaking of works by a former chairman of the Art Department, Raymond MacMahon, now retired. Conversations with Ray are among the most cherished memories from my eight years as chaplain of the college, and I like to sit here and remember those days.

Some folks see these paintings as hard and cold. Most are composed of enamel paint on masonite, a synthetic board with a smooth surface and, typically, the paintings have only two or three colors. And their angular shapes do not remind you of anything you are familiar with. People would come to gallery openings and, after looking at one of these works briefly, would ask the artist, "What is it?" And he would reply, "It is a painting." But what is it a painting *of*, they would want to know. In Ray's view, such questions reveal that the viewer thinks of a painting as a window; you look through it to see something else, something you can recognize. I think that is why he eventually stopped painting on surfaces that were square or rectangular, making it harder to imagine that his paintings are like windows which enable you to see something other than themselves.

The artist Frank Stella once said, "What you see is what you see." These paintings celebrate the act of seeing. If you look at one for a while, the background will become the foreground and vice versa. In that sense the paintings appear to move. Ray referred to this phenomenon as "equivocal space." These paintings are therefore not really cold and hard; they are, rather, playful and celebratory. We can see! This is art that invites us, perhaps requires us, to see what is in our line of vision, to see what is actually there before us. If we can learn how to see one of Ray MacMahon's paintings there is no telling what else we might see in the world around us. I can't visit this place without feeling a surge of gratitude for one who gave me an extraordinary gift: he helped me learn how to see and that one thing has enriched my life.

This college itself has greatly enriched my life. Here I learned not only to see, but also to think. As odd as it may sound, we have to learn how to think. That is to say that we have to become aware of the process of thinking, just as we need to pay attention to the process of seeing. We have a moral obligation to think critically, to be able better to judge what is true and what is false, what is right and what is wrong. I could name many more gifts this college has given me: listening, speaking, and a love of reading come to mind immediately. But I will just say that, had I not been a student here my life would have been very different. I am a child of this "fostering mother," my alma mater. And, sitting here today in the autumn of my life, I look back with profound gratitude.

Birmingham-Southern College, Birmingham, Alabama, 2003

Acknowledgements

As I said in the introduction, the kind of writing I have done in this book originally grew out of my youthful struggle to prepare sermons long before the age when anyone should have such a responsibility week after week. But, having lived through that time and all the years since I am glad that I faced such a challenge so early in my life. I could not begin to count or even remember all the people who, from the start, gave me encouragement both as a preacher and as a writer. The late Howard Thurman, who read some of the early prayers and urged me to continue writing them certainly strengthened my confidence, as did Professor Bill Huntley when he invited me to read them before a town and gown audience at the University of Redlands. And I owe much to Professor Luther E. Smith who read this manuscript at an early stage of its development and made many helpful suggestions as well as urging me to seek a publisher.

On more than one occasion I have shared selections from this book with Janet Cromwell of the School of Theology at Claremont and received spirit-lifting responses in return. My secretary at Emory, Stella Feagle, who occasionally typed some of this material, continually encouraged me to keep on writing. And I am particularly grateful to John Collett, pastor of the Belmont United Methodist Church in Nashville, who commended my work to a potential publisher after hearing me read some of the prayers at a luncheon at the church.

I cannot begin to thank all the people whose participation and support meant so much to me as I offered leadership in campus chapels. It would be a mistake for me to single out any one of them, but I do want to say to any who may chance to read these words that their kind words of support were critically important to me. I mention the chapel congregations because, in several cases, they were the first to hear these private prayers read aloud.

The opinions I trust the most are those of my immediate family and closest friends. I'm afraid that I have thrust my writing upon them a little too much at times, but they have regularly given me their blessing and encouraged me to continue. My strongest supporter, who is also less reluctant than any other to tell me when I have missed the mark, is my wife, Mary Jim. Her advice has been important at every step of the way with respect to any project I have ever attempted, this one not least of all. She knows that I would be utterly lost without her daily companionship and conversation about everything that concerns either of us.

The excerpt from *The Seven Storey Mountain* by Thomas Merton, copyright 1948 by Harcourt, Inc. and renewed 1976 by the Trustees of The Merton Legacy Trust is reprinted by permission of the publisher. The brief excerpt used as an epigraph at the beginning is from *A Listening Heart* by David Steindl-Rast, published by Crossroad Publishing Company in 1983. The excerpt from Truman Capote is from *A Christmas Memory*, published by Random House (Modern Library Edition, 1996).

Anyone who has read this far will know how profoundly my consciousness has been shaped by hymns. In the section, "Are You Security?" I quoted the first stanza of "I Am Thine, O Lord" by Fanny J. Crosby, and I referred to it again in "New York: the Beginner." In the piece, "Evening Lamps" I quoted a stanza from "Day Is Dying in the West" by Mary A. Lathbury. There is a brief reference to Maltbie D. Babcock's "This Is My Father's World" in "Something To Declare." All of these old hymns may be found in the 1966 edition of *The Cokesbury Worship Hymnal* published by Abingdon Press. The hymn "Praise, My Soul, the King of Heaven" by Henry F. Lyte, also quoted in "Something To Declare," may be found in *The Book of Hymns* published by The United Methodist Publishing House in 1966.

The song "Alabama Bound" in the section of the same name is believed to have been written many years ago by the director and members of the Warbler's Club at Woodlawn High School in Birmingham. I have been unable to determine if it was ever published. I do know that it is not from a song of the same name in the blues genre.

Finally, this book is dedicated to the memory of one of my best friends, Jim Ifft. He had as much zest for life as anyone I have ever known, making it much harder to have him leave us while still in his forties. He and his wife Evelyn had two sons and a daughter, as did Mary Jim and I. All of us spent many happy hours together in the mountains, on the beach and in our backyards and family rooms. As Professor of Chemistry and Dean of Natural Sciences at the University of Redlands, Jim was an extraordinarily effective teacher whether the subject was chemistry, wine-making or fly fishing. He was an avid outdoorsman and a person of deep faith who loved it when we all sang "Amazing Grace" whether in church or before an open fire on a winter evening. I think he would be pleased to know how vividly and gratefully he is remembered.